# BEFORE YOU START READING, DOWNLOAD YOUR FREE BONUSES!

Scan the QR-code & Access
all the  Resources for FREE!

SCAN ME

## The Self-Sufficient Living Cheat Sheet

## 10 Simple Steps to Become More Self-Sufficient in 1 Hour or Less

How to restore balance to the environment around you... even if you live in a tiny apartment in the city.

Discover:

- **How to increase your income** by selling "useless" household items
- The environmentally friendly way to replace your car — invest in THIS special vehicle to **eliminate your carbon footprint**
- The secret ingredient to **turning your backyard into a thriving garden**
- 17+ different types of food scraps and 'waste' that you can use to feed your garden
- How to drastically **cut down on food waste** without eating less
- 4 natural products you can use to make your own eco-friendly cleaning supplies
- The simple alternative to 'consumerism' — the age-old method for **getting what you need without paying money for it**
- The 9 fundamental items you need to create a self-sufficient first-aid kit
- One of the top skills that most people are afraid of learning — and how you can master it effortlessly
- 3 essential tips for **gaining financial independence**

## The Prepper Emergency Preparedness & Survival Checklist:

## 10 Easy Things You Can Do Right Now to Ready Your Family & Home for Any Life-Threatening Catastrophe

**Natural disasters demolish everything in their path, but your peace of mind and sense of safety don't have to be among them. Here's what you need to know...**

- Why having an emergency plan in place is so crucial and how it will help to keep your family safe
- How to stockpile emergency supplies intelligently and why you shouldn't overdo it
- How to store and conserve water so that you know you'll have enough to last you through the crisis
- A powerful 3-step guide to ensuring financial preparedness, no matter what happens
- A step-by-step guide to maximizing your storage space, so you and your family can have exactly what you need ready and available at all times
- Why knowing the hazards of your home ahead of time could save a life and how to steer clear of these in case of an emergency
- Everything you need to know for creating a successful evacuation plan, should the worst happen and you need to flee safely

## 101 Recipes, Tips, Crafts, DIY Projects and More for a Beautiful Low Waste Life

## Reduce Your Carbon Footprint and Make Earth-Friendly Living Fun With This Comprehensive Guide

Practical, easy ways to improve your personal health and habits while contributing to a brighter future for yourself and the planet

Discover:

- **Simple customizable recipes for creating your own food, home garden, and skincare products**

- The tools you need for each project to successfully achieve sustainable living

- Step-by-step instructions for life-enhancing skills from preserving food to raising your own animals and forging for wild berries

- **Realistic life changes that reduce your carbon-footprint while saving you money**

- Sustainable crafts that don't require any previous knowledge or expertise

- Self-care that extends beyond the individual and positively impacts the environment

- **Essential tips on how to take back control of your life -- become self-sustained and independent**

# First Aid Fundamentals

## A Step-By-Step Illustrated Guide to the Top 10 Essential First Aid Procedures Everyone Should Know

Discover:

- **What you should do to keep this type of animal attack from turning into a fatal allergic reaction**

- Why sprains are more than just minor injuries, and how you can keep them from getting worse

- **How to make the best use of your environment in critical situations**

- The difference between second- and third-degree burns, and what you should do when either one happens

- Why treating a burn with ice can actually cause more damage to your skin

- When to use heat to treat an injury, and when you should use something cold

- **How to determine the severity of frostbite**, and what you should do in specific cases

- Why knowing this popular disco song could help you save a life

- The key first aid skill that everyone should know — **make sure you learn THIS technique the right way**

## Food Preservation Starter Kit

## 10 Beginner-Friendly Ways to Preserve Food at Home | Including Instructional Illustrations and Simple Directions

Grocery store prices are skyrocketing! It's time for a self-sustaining lifestyle.

Discover:

- **10 incredibly effective and easy ways to preserve your food for a self-sustaining lifestyle**

- The art of canning and the many different ways you can preserve food efficiently without any prior experience

- A glorious trip down memory lane to learn the historical methods of preservation passed down from one generation to the next

- **How to make your own pickled goods**: enjoy the tanginess straight from your kitchen

- Detailed illustrations and directions so you won't feel lost in the preservation process

- The health benefits of dehydrating your food and how fermentation can be **the key to a self-sufficient life**

- **The secrets to living a processed-free life** and saving Mother Earth all at the same time

# Download all your resources by scanning the QR-Code below:

# HOW TO START A 501(C)(3) NONPROFIT

*Step-By-Step Guide To Legally Start, Grow
and Run Your Own Non Profit in as Little as
30 Days While Avoiding the Common Pitfalls
That New Startups Encounter*

By Small Footprint Press

# Table of Contents

# Introduction

*"We make a living by what we get, we make a life by what we give."*

*Winston Churchill*

Nonprofits are tax-exempt organizations that operate to bring results that benefit a community. That could be fighting animal cruelty, promoting sports and education among youth, or offering low-cost dental health. These are specific examples, but they give a good overview of the different roles a nonprofit can assume.

Nonprofits are born from the desire of people who want to see a change and aren't satisfied with donating or offering volunteer work to pre-existing organizations. Instead, they want to be leaders and advocate the causes that are dear to them.

Many nonprofits are born from people who lived in disadvantaged communities but were able to get education and work experience. So they create their own organizations to help people in similar situations as a way of giving members of that community the same extraordinary chances that they had.

We all have a desire to change the world, but few people do something about it. If you are unsatisfied with the way things are and want to do something more than complain, more power to you, but you should be prepared for a lot of difficulties on your way. There's a reason people sit down and complain: it's easy. Running an enterprise dedicated to improving the lives of people around you is much harder.

Creating and running a nonprofit is a life-changing experience that involves a lot of rewarding work and the satisfaction of helping others. But you must treat it with seriousness and respect. Otherwise, your organization could be doomed before it starts.

A lot of things can go wrong when you're trying to do right by people. Creating and running a nonprofit involves an astounding amount of paperwork, and that can scare away people who are only interested in the practical side. You will be spending a lot of time filling out forms to ensure that your organization keeps its tax-exempt status. You will also have to hire and monitor people, including board members, staff, and volunteers.

Think of it as opening a bookstore. You could be an avid reader who knows all the classics and can recite Shakespeare and Dostoyevsky by heart. You then decide it's time to take your love one step forward and start sharing your love with others.

You raise some money and open a bookstore, and the problems arise. First, you need to hire people, something you never did before. So, you decide to give a job to your nephew, who you can depend on.

You'll also be in charge of shipping. Buying and selling books is like any other merchandise: you look for book distributors to bring shipments to you, but you don't know how much that should cost, and you have the possibility of getting ripped off. In addition, shipments may sometimes get delayed, and you don't receive any of the newest editions for your clients.

Speaking of clients, they are not that many, and some of them aren't as interested in the classics as you are. Still, with every penny you get, you use it to improve your book store. You may not have gotten as rich you could from your business if you were operating in another way, but you're doing something you believe in and love. And you do it for the kind of people who feel the same way.

Nonprofits operate in a similar and special way. Apart from the salary given to the staff, any revenue that is made from the organization's work is used to improve their programs. The goal is to always improve the projects of the organization, to make them more accessible to the public, to get better equipment, and hire more personnel who can help them.

What would motivate anyone or even you to start an enterprise like that? Maybe you've been feeling frustrated with the current situations you see in the world or your area. Perhaps coming from a poor neighborhood, you decided to open a nonprofit that would benefit the kids who will grow up in the same streets. Maybe you lost someone to a sickness, and now you're inspired to create a foundation that would help people that also have it. Or lastly, maybe you want to use it to promote yourself in the eyes of the community while also helping people to improve their situation.

If you are going to open a nonprofit to advocate a cause you're passionate about, you must look at it objectively. Treat this as a business, but also keep the flame of that passion alive. A lot of the work in a nonprofit is executed by volunteers, people who will donate their most precious commodity: time. They do that because they believe in a cause, not because they expect anything in return. So be the person who inspires them to follow that cause.

While it can be dangerous to keep a fully romantic view of your nonprofit, this is a field that requires idealism. People who decide to choose nonprofit as a career need to have courage, resilience, and tenacity. You're not working only to collect a paycheck at the end of the month. Your organization and the project it will arrange will hopefully be the reason that many people's lives will change.

Jim Ziolkowski is the founder of a nonprofit called buildOn, which runs after-school programs for impoverished children in the U.S., and builds schools in developing countries. To achieve that on a global scale, they count on an army of volunteers who want to turn the world into a better place. The bureaucracy that goes on behind the organization isn't what attracts these volunteers; the picture of a starving child being served healthy and abundant meals is.

A nonprofit needs to have a defined purpose that will guide all its actions. An organization cannot solve all the problems of your community. You should focus on specific issues and demographics rather than juggling several matters and getting none of them right.

To run a nonprofit the right way, you need to get a 501(c)(3) tax exemption. Getting that exemption is hard enough, and keeping it can be a nightmare. The finances of your nonprofit will be open to public scrutiny, and you must send several forms throughout the year to keep that status. In addition, a small mistake made by your staff or board members, whether intentional or not, can doom your organization.

So that you can keep your nonprofit working in the long term, it will be crucial for you to maintain financial accountability and control over your revenue. The IRS is strict when it comes to monitoring nonprofit's finances, so you must take this seriously. Even if you have a great vision, a solid working model, and a dedicated staff, your financial management should be at the top of your priorities.

If this entire process sounds overwhelming, we have great news for you: by acquiring this book, you have received a helpful guide on how to go through all of it. In these pages, we'll walk you through the entire path of figuring out exactly what you want to accomplish with your projects. Then we'll help you look for the best way to implement those ideas and arrange the necessary forms to stay up-to-date with the IRS, protecting and growing your nonprofit, all while keeping the main mission of your nonprofit in your heart and mind.

You cannot run a nonprofit on your own, so you should be able to select the people who will commit and be by your side. These people will be the ones to help raise money for your organization, implement programs, train volunteers, represent your nonprofit to the public, identify needs in the community, and do everyday work such as answering the phone. We'll show you how to select and hire the people, even if you don't have an HR background.

Taking care of your budget can be tricky. Still, we'll help you use tools such as core numbers, cash flow forecast, statement of activity, and functional expenses, and filling in Form 990—the most important form for a nonprofit. We will also go through the different computer systems you can use to make your organization run smoothly.

At the end of this book, we will offer links for you to access the most important forms that you'll need to start and manage your nonprofit. The instructions on how and when to fill these forms will be included throughout the book. Of course, you can fill in a lot of the paperwork yourself, but it's always wise to have a lawyer or accountant examine these documents before you file them.

**About Small Footprint Press**

"Accelerating Sustainable Survival for the Individual and our Planet." -. Small Footprint Press

We were born out of frustration with the current state of the world and the environment. We believe in giving power back to the individual while taking care of our planet, that is the only way to survive in the long run. For this reason, we work toward promoting and encouraging sustainable living as an individual. By providing resources for those inspired to change their situations, achieve self-sufficiency, live off the grid, or be prepared for the worst, we have been able to change lives step by step. We wrote this book as a mission to help you jumpstart your mission on creating a successful nonprofit organization. What you're about to learn will help you to avoid the usual issues that many other people have struggled with when running a nonprofit. Some of these problems you can only foresee once you've actually experienced owning a nonprofit yourself.

Creating and running a nonprofit organization is an act of love, and it brings out the best in people. We want to share the knowledge of creating organizations like this from beginning to end and how to keep it from closing its doors before it can fulfill its mission.

Nonprofits are here to make that change. According to the National Council of Profits, every person in the country has been benefited somehow by the work of a nonprofit, whether they realize it or not. But, of course, this happens in extreme situations, like getting aid during a disaster or even just learning how to tie a knot in your childhood as a boy scout.

In this book, we will be learning the different definitions of nonprofits, the meaning of the 501(c)(3) status, and what separates these organizations from not-for-profits and for-profits. There are several perks to running a nonprofit, but there are also some disadvantages, all of which we'll dive into.

We'll then be ready to start looking into the practical side of things. This involves funding your operation and putting together your team. We'll see what makes a good board, as well as how to get the best staff of paid employees and volunteers.

Your nonprofit should have a catchy name, and in this next chapter, we will be helping you with how you can create your own. We'll also see the process of becoming tax-exempt and how to keep the 501(c)(3) status.

It's no good to have a fully functioning nonprofit that nobody knows exists. So you should also make sure you create a functioning website and use social media to gather donors and grants. It's also crucial to have a good software system, which we'll explain in detail in Chapter 4. That system should help you communicate internally and externally and organize your documents and finances.

In Chapter 5, we will present to you the most important document you need to fill to keep your tax exemption: Form 990. This is an annual form that you must submit to the IRS showing that you are conducting your finances in the proper way. This chapter will also deal with conflicts of interest, which could damage your most important activities.

In order to make sure that your nonprofit is achieving its goals, you must create and monitor the programs that you implement. In Chapter 7, we will be dealing with strategic planning, program identity, the way you deliver your services, and the way you evaluate the success of a program implemented by your organization.

Chapter 7 is about risk management, that is, foreseeing everything that could go wrong. We'll talk about the importance of insurance coverage, including the different types of policies you could get. We'll also use this chapter to discuss the importance of valuing your staff while growing your nonprofit.

Chapter 8 will include several form templates that you can use in your daily activities. We also included a few lists of instructions that will help you to write your own documents from scratch. These don't replace the assistance you could get by hiring an accountant or an attorney, but they should be helpful when you're starting out.

Knowing how to start a 501(c)(3) nonprofit, with all its challenges and rewards, is the basis of creating genuine change. You have decided to face these challenges, and this guide is going to be your weapon to deal with the obstacles in your path. This knowledge is now yours. Use it wisely.

# Chapter 1:
# Why Start a Nonprofit

## Nonprofit Vs. Not-For-Profit Vs. For-Profits

Creating and running a nonprofit is a serious business, and that's how it should be treated. Entrepreneurship is key in that regard, and the members of the nonprofit organization should have the skills to keep it running. Having a staff that loves what they're doing is essential, but it's also necessary to have people who know what they're doing.

The significant difference with a nonprofit is the sense of mission. In a profit-oriented company, everyone is working to make money for the investors. People don't work for an accounting firm out of their love for accounting as a tool to make a better society. They do it because they want to support their families and repay the trust of the people who hired them.

A nonprofit organization runs better when everyone working in it shares that same sense of mission and will give their best to make it work. There's a wide range of missions that these companies can work for, but, as the name says, they're not interested in making anyone richer. For a nonprofit to assure that, they don't have a single owner. Instead, they are run by a board of directors with at least three people in order to distribute the financial responsibilities.

The primary goal isn't to gain profit for the shareholders but to make sure that the company is providing the services for those who need them. For example, a nonprofit uses the money it makes to pay the employees and increase their services. The success of the profit is based on the success of its mission. The more people are benefited from its services, the more successful it is.

Why go through the trouble of creating and running an organization that won't generate any profit? People build nonprofits for many reasons. One of them is creating something larger that can impact other people's lives. Not only will you help the people being attended by the organization but also the volunteers and employees who can make something meaningful with their time.

The staff of a nonprofit, be it paid employees or volunteers, all come together to fulfill the nonprofit's mission. That could be feeding the homeless, running an abandoned animal shelter, or running a free dentistry clinic. But, of course, that doesn't mean people can't get a good income working for nonprofits. Still, there are many ways of securing money for the company and its employees through fundraising and sponsorships.

Being a board member of a nonprofit can give you a place in history. While other sorts of businesses generate more wealth in comparison, nonprofits have a lasting impact in preserving their creators' names in people's minds. People also create nonprofits to pay tribute to the memory of a deceased loved one. Creating an organization with that person's name that will honor a cause that was dear to them in life is a way of keeping the flame of that person alive.

Before creating a nonprofit, it's crucial to have a defined goal. For example, the purpose of a law firm is to offer people legal services for money. Likewise, the purpose of a pizza place is to provide people with high-quality pizza so that they'll keep coming back and paying for more. But if profit isn't your goal, then what is?

Your company is going to function with grants and donations. Whether these donations are public or private, from companies or individuals, you will need to be transparent about how this money is being used. And to be transparent, you need to give people a good reason why you need their money.

There are many ways of getting donations that can range from filling in online forms to get grants (both public and private) or running campaigns on social media. If these processes overwhelm you, don't be afraid to look for help. That could be a lawyer who can teach you how to get tax exemption or a YouTuber with thousands of followers who could speak about your nonprofit in one of his videos.

The workforce of a nonprofit is composed of paid employees and volunteers, the former usually assisting the latter. Volunteers work for a cause, but also to get credits at university and work experience. The paid employees' salary always comes from the revenue created by the company's activities, never from donations.

Nonprofit organizations 501(c)(3), such as national foundations, charities, hospitals, and universities, qualify for tax-exempt status by the IRS. That's because their entire profit is reabsorbed to further the organization's agenda of fostering a social cause and improving the community.

Because of that tax exemption, these organizations are regulated by strict rules regarding the activities they provide. No private individual can be unfairly benefitted by the net earnings of a nonprofit, which should all go to charitable purposes. In case the organization ceases to exist, all the money that remains after paying its debts must be used for charitable purposes.

The advancement of the organization's mission is the pillar of a nonprofit. Thus, any profit should be used only to advance that mission. They are also prohibited from endorsing political campaigns and conducting political lobbying or propaganda. Unfortunately, there are organizations that engage in such activities, and which are considered nonprofit, but that don't meet the IRS standards and therefore don't qualify for tax exemption.

Most religious organizations qualify as nonprofits, for they are usually organized around their faith. Apart from the religious ceremonies, they also conduct activities to get new converts and help people in the community. Community theaters, dance companies, and orchestras can also apply for a tax exemption as nonprofits 501(c)(3), as well as museums and chambers of commerce and boards.

It's not uncommon for for-profit organizations to create related nonprofit 501(c)(3) as a way of providing charitable work free of tax. In addition, celebrities, such as athletes, film actors, and actresses, have 501(c)(3) foundations created on their names as a way of giving back for their success.

The IRS has a list of types of tax-exempt profits that include organizations dedicated to exempt purposes. Exempt purposes can be charitable, literary, educational, religious, scientific, or dedicated to fighting the mistreatment of children and animals. In addition, private foundations, which are usually created by families, and are dedicated to donating money and resources to other nonprofits, also qualify as exempt purposes.

Being exempt from taxes helps nonprofits to survive economically. Otherwise, they would have to spend a good chunk of their revenue to pay for the property taxes alone, and that money wouldn't be used for the company's mission. Donations can also be itemized on taxes, which is an excellent incentive for people to contribute to the cause.

The IRS also requires that nonprofits have a gift acceptance policy. While some gifts are reasonable to accept, others can lead to legal issues and damage the name of the nonprofit. A reasonable example would be someone donating a vehicle to a nonprofit that distributes food in impoverished regions. That vehicle could fulfill the organization's purposes, which wouldn't be the case if the gift was an old painting or a statue.

## Nonprofit Vs. Not-for-Profit Vs. For-Profits

It's a common mistake to think that nonprofit and not-for-profit are two names for the same thing. The names seem to imply that they are simply the reverse of for-profit companies. Instead, nonprofits and not-for-profits are two different business structures that involve distinct governances and functions regarding their taxes.

As we've seen, nonprofit organizations 501(c)(3) qualify for tax exemption because of their mission to benefit the public. In a nutshell, these are companies that serve the public good and are eligible for that exemption so they can continue to fulfill that mission. To do that, they must keep their operations and financial information public, allowing the donors to see the results of their contributions. Therefore, these contributions are also tax-deductible.

The first thing that differentiates the not-for-profit 501(c) is that they don't always work for the benefit of the community and can serve the private purposes of their members. A local baseball club or homeowner's association, for example, doesn't operate to create revenue for its owners. In that case, all money that's earned—be it through donations or the activities themselves—is used to better run the organization. Not-for-profits can apply for tax exemption, but in this case, the money that's donated to them cannot be deducted from the donor.

Nonprofits can be associated with separate legal entities, unlike not-for-profits. Another difference is that running a nonprofit has more to do with running a business with paid employees, while a not-for-profit is seen as a recreational entity by its members. While nonprofits have a share of volunteers working for them, the members of not-for-profits work entirely on a volunteer basis.

It's possible for a nonprofit to change its mission statements at any point if the new mission still qualifies for a tax-exempt status under section 501(c)(3). You should inform the IRS before doing so, or else you could jeopardize your organization's task exemption.

## The Differences Between a 501(c)(3) & Other Nonprofit Organization

State laws govern the process of becoming a nonprofit, even though it will affect your federal tax bills. This is because nonprofits are corporations, which need to be registered at a state level. The IRS will check your documentation to see if your company qualifies as a 501(c)(3).

Getting tax exemption is an arduous process, but it becomes less complicated when you understand what type of nonprofit you're creating. The IRS offers precise definitions for these organizations. For example, the broad definition of 501(c)(3) is charities, and it requires a different IRS requirement process than other 501(c) categories.

Charities are organizations dedicated to improving the living conditions of people in a community and helping those in need. The work of a charity can involve, for example, a restaurant dedicated to offering good quality food at low prices for people living in a poor neighborhood or a charity clinic that offers treatment for people with HIV. They can also work in the building and maintenance of monuments, defending human rights, fighting discrimination, helping the poor advancing education, fostering amateur sports, etc.

Charities of all kinds are entitled to the 501(c)(3) status, which provides tax exemption. They get their funding for soliciting donations to their community and crowdfunding on the internet but can also have bigger sources of funding coming from a wealthy benefactor, a heritage, or a private foundation.

While all charities are nonprofits, some nonprofits are not charities. For example, a veteran association can't be considered a charity, but it can still help the community by helping people with PTSD to reintegrate. Likewise, a parent association isn't a charity either but can be considered a nonprofit if it serves the community by improving the education in a public school. Other kinds of nonprofits that are not charities include chambers of commerce, teachers' retirement fund associations, labor, agricultural, and horticultural organizations, among others.

# Types of 501(c)(3) Organizations

There are three primary categories for 501(c)(3) organizations: public charities, private foundations, and private operating foundations.

The most well-known are public charities, organizations that are dedicated to the benefit of the public. They act in a plethora of fields, using different methods. Public charities get a good chunk of their finance from donations from the public and funding programs for the government. It's mandatory that at least one-third of the revenue of a public charity must come from donations from the public. An individual donor can get a tax-deductible up to 60% of his income from these donations. Cooperative donors can get up to 10%.

Private foundations are charity companies that don't conduct operations or programs themselves. Instead, they work to support the programs of other charities. Because of that, they are known as non-operating foundations. The revenue of these foundations can come from a small group of individual donors.

Private foundations can be run by small groups of people or even families. If, for example, a family loses a young daughter who dreamt of becoming a medical doctor, they can create a private foundation in her name to offer scholarships to young girls with the same dream.

Donating to a private foundation allows a tax deduction of up to 30% of the donor's income. In addition, a private foundation's board has fewer members than other nonprofits, which means its governance can be held more closely.

Private operating foundations are rarer. They can be considered an amalgam of the two previous ones, conducting activities like charities while having governance that gets them closer to a private foundation. At least 85% of the income must be spent on exempt activities, and they are entitled to the same amount of tax exemption as charities.

## Is a Nonprofit Right for You and Your Goals?

Nonprofits are special organizations that operate in a specific way and with a specific set of rules. For example, opening an organization to offer food to the homeless will involve a distinct set of skills than opening a restaurant. We've seen some benefits and disadvantages of running such an enterprise, so the question now is if this model of business is right for you.

Having this book in your hands is a good sign you're on the right path. Before starting a nonprofit, it's important to do the proper research. It's crucial that you know what you're getting into and the many difficulties that will be appearing in your path. Ask yourself what you want to achieve, figure how you want to achieve it, and find out all you can beforehand.

Getting that information is important not only to know how to run a nonprofit but also to learn if you should create one. There are many ways of doing good for the community, and creating a charity is just one of them. Some people have done plenty of good with individual actions, or even through for-profits.

Ask yourself if you could achieve what you want while running a for-profit. To go back to the last example: could you open a restaurant, make a profit out of it, and use some of that profit to offer food to the homeless? You might not be feeding as many people but would still do good and make a profit at the same time.

Running a nonprofit can be expensive. Every dollar you raise must be used for the organization, and that means paying rent, electricity and water bills, the employee's salary, and legal fees. With so many charity foundations operating across the country, fundraising has become an arduous activity. The 501(c)(3) status doesn't mean that their finances are a breeze, especially considering that they depend on these donations to have an income while also being under constant scrutiny.

Asking people to share a portion of their money with your organization works better if you are defending a cause that they care about. Most donors don't really care about the tax exemption: they want to help a cause that they can relate to. Keep in good relations with these donors because they will be the ones who will pay your bills, and you can't sue them if they decide to stop giving.

If you decide not to start a nonprofit, there are still many ways to do good and help a cause. The most obvious ones are donating to an existing nonprofit and offering voluntary service. Volunteering can be done online or in person, and donations can be in cash or other goods, such as old books or food. Nonprofits need that help to survive and will welcome your contribution.

While opening a new nonprofit can be tricky, you can also open a chapter of an existing one that aligns with your values. After getting permission from the parent organization, you can open an affiliate that works like a franchise. The parent organization will let you use their copyrighted name and work to spread their values. Your chapter will have limited access to the funds of the parent organization, but you will also have access to their 501(c)(3) status.

Setting up a for-profit business that helps support nonprofits can be as rewarding as running a nonprofit. We've already mentioned the restaurant example, but this can also be a bookshop that donates part of its revenue to an educational fund or a secondhand clothes shop that donates coats to the homeless. Even if you don't own a business, you can set up a donation cycle among your friends and family to help one or several charities with money.

## Benefits of a Nonprofit

Building a nonprofit starts with an idea but requires much more than that to succeed. However, with focus and persistence, it's possible to turn that idea into something more. The benefits of creating and running a 501(c)(3) go far beyond the tax exemption status. Here are some of them:

## Limited Liability

The risks involved in starting a nonprofit are considerably small compared to a small for-profit business. While the owners of a for-profit are often associated with the company, a nonprofit is considered a separate entity from the individuals running it. Therefore, many of the legal matters that would negatively impact the proprietor or partner of a for-profit business don't have the same impact on the board members of a nonprofit.

Nonprofits are protected by the law against creditors and courts. People involved in funding, financing, and running the nonprofit hold no personal liability in the company's debt. That, of course, doesn't mean a person can use their work on a nonprofit as a shield to commit illegal acts. Also, directors can be held liable if, through their actions or inaction, the nonprofit suffers any loss.

## Separation of the Nonprofit and Individuals

An individual's legal issues can affect the running of a profit. Nonprofits, however, are in a public domain and remain unharmed by their runners' legal issues. They legally have an existence of their own and can conduct their own legal matters, such as entering a contract or taking part in a sue, without impacting its owners.

## *Funding Eligibility*

Nonprofits may receive grants from both the public and private sectors. Many grants are available solely for public charities and can't be claimed by for-profits. Federal grants are funded with taxpayer money and therefore are aimed at organizations with exempt purposes.

Tax deductions are available for individuals and businesses that offer donations to nonprofit charities.

## *Credibility*

Creating and running a nonprofit increases the credibility of its owners in the community. A company or person also donates their credibility to the nonprofit they're running. For example, people will be more inclined to make donations to a nonprofit that's run by a company they have known for years rather than one that they have never heard of.

## *Postage Discounts*

Nonprofits also come with reduced rates on postal services. For example, their printed material can be mailed as USPS Marketing Mail, with a significant discount. Other materials, such as bills and statements of accounts, as well as handwritten or typewritten material, are not eligible for this service.

## Disadvantages of a Nonprofit

Running a nonprofit isn't easy and can also have negative impacts on your professional life. However, knowing what these advantages are will help you decide if you should really embark on this journey or try something different.

### *Loads of Paperwork*

Any business has paperwork, but with tax-exempt companies, you must pay special attention to it. It's advisable to keep specific records of all activities conducted by the charity daily. The IRS always has an eye on nonprofits to guarantee that they will keep fulfilling their exempt purposes. Because of that, all 501(c)(3) organizations must submit their records to the IRS on specific deadlines to keep that status.

### *Public Scrutiny*

Being exempt from taxes means that the finances of a nonprofit must be open to the public. Charities are supposed to work for the public, and that data is considered public interest. Therefore, copies of documents detailing the organization's state and operations, including salaries, should be available for anyone who asks for it.

### *Costly Fees*

Again, any business must deal with fees for accounting, renting, furniture, legal counseling, and other activities. It's also necessary to pay for the application of tax exemption and incorporation with other organizations. With a charity organization, it's necessary to keep in mind that the money spent won't generate profit later. It's wise to create a budget beforehand to know what you're getting into.

## *Shared Control*

You won't have as much personal control in a 501(c)(3) as in a for-profit. The number of laws and regulations involved—including self-regulation and bylaws—can be overwhelming, and some states require that nonprofits have more than one director. That board of directors will vote for the most important decisions, and the majority must be respected.

## *Lack of Profit*

If you can't accept the fact that you will not make a profit while running a nonprofit, that's a sign you should rethink your priorities. The only money you can make from your work at a 501(c)(3) is in the fixed salary, and all the revenue created by the company's activities must be reabsorbed and used to improve those activities.

Any unrelated income that's created and not reabsorbed will catch the attention of the IRS, and you might lose your exempt status and must pay a fine. In addition, you can't use the assets of a nonprofit, including the workforce of its staff, to create other income-producing activities.

When a nonprofit must close its doors, the resources left must pay its creditors. Whatever money is left from the organization needs to be donated to other charitable groups. The owners and board of directors are forbidden by law to pocket that money.

A 501(c)(3) founder is entitled to a reasonable compensation for their work in the profit. However, be careful not to pay yourself more than the basis of reasonableness established by the IRS. That number is established in the organization budget compared to the number of worked hours, the average compensation in the area, and your level of education. More than that could jeopardize your exempt status.

Some ways of generating related income are:

- Renting out space to professionals who have a similar cause—for example, renting an auditorium for a public speaker.

- Consulting or facilitating training. Use the knowledge that you and your staff gathered as a way of making revenue for your nonprofit.

- Licensing intellectual property created by your nonprofit. The same knowledge you used to provide consultancy, for example, could be used to write a book on how to run a similar organization.

- Selling products that are related to your cause, such as items with your logo in them, is an excellent marketing strategy and a way of making money.

- Developing a social enterprise, such as a Limited Liability Company (LLC), which is a company with the same structure as a for-profit, but with a mission like a nonprofit.

The IRS has regulations keeping nonprofits from generating too much income. All related income should be aligned with the nonprofit's main mission. Any profit that doesn't fit that description is considered unrelated income. In order not to jeopardize your 501(c)(3) status, the unrelated income should not amount to more than $1,000.00.

# Chapter 2:
# Establishing Your Vision

Another aspect in which running a nonprofit differs from a for-profit is the sense of purpose. If you are not running this company to fill your pockets with money, why are you running it for? If you must go through all the bureaucracy and spend all that money, there must be some sort of compensation at the end, right?

The focus of a nonprofit is to gather people and resources to fight for one common cause. This could be preserving the environment, fighting animal cruelty and child abuse, promoting education, or advancing science and research for the common good. Choosing that goal is the first step to creating a nonprofit. Then, the organization should know what they're fighting for when the time comes to raise money.

When someone donates money for a nonprofit, they want to see that money being spent to advance that cause. If the organization changes the cause at some point, the donors are likely to lessen. Because of that, nonprofits need to be transparent and show how that money is being spent.

Donations don't always come as money. Many people choose to help nonprofits with volunteer work. That work could be something specialized, such as accounting, but it can also come from people without a degree who want to help by doing more mundane tasks. Volunteer work is precious for nonprofits and knowing how to gather it is key in making the organization work.

Having a clear purpose will also give the staff and volunteers a solid base to work on and keep them motivated. It's crucial that they relate to that cause. Recruiting people that are part of the demographic benefited by the nonprofit's mission is a good way of keeping them motivated.

It's important to create a mission statement that will define the work and vision that's being implemented. That statement should be short and clear and define the reasons your nonprofit exists. A well-crafted statement will be the guide that keeps everyone focused and communicates that vision to potential collaborators.

Those contributions are the basis for the functioning of a nonprofit. Not only do they provide resources, both tangible and intangible, but they also build a positive image amongst the general public, strengthening ties with the community.

## What Makes an Ideal Nonprofit?

Knowing what you want to achieve is the first step. Now it's time to shape that idea into the real world. A great way of knowing if your idea is viable is to conduct a needs assessment to collect data about your target audience.

This study will give you an idea if the resources you have are enough to fulfill the community's needs. Then, with that data in hand, you can start planning how much you'll need in donations and the needed staff of employees and volunteers.

Write the characteristics of an ideal supporter of your organization, including age, education, work experience, and income. Then, figure out what motivates that ideal person to donate for you and have that in mind when selecting people to request donations. Of course, you might never find a person who ticks every box on the list, but this is a good starting point.

The needs assessment is also useful to find out what other organizations are already doing in the field you plan to work. You can do that by simply talking to people who work at other nonprofits and businesses with similar missions. That could lead you to revise your initial ideas, which is better to do at this stage.

Knocking at people's doors and asking questions can be just as useful. It's great for finding out about the services provided by nonprofits from the other side of the matter. To go the extra mile, visit other places and find out about how nonprofits are acting in their community, so you can apply the ideas to your work.

It's important that you research logistics and practicalities, such as federal, state, and local laws, that will influence your work. For example, you can find basic demographic information about your area in the U.S. Census Bureau, and knowing how to interpret those laws will allow you to plan.

The people who are working for you, being paid or not, need to trust your integrity and believe that you are doing what's best for the organization and the community. Don't compromise that trust, for it's the pillar of any nonprofit. Always pass the image of someone who's committed to doing good, and you'll inspire these people to do the same.

It can be hard to focus on the major picture when you must defeat the challenges of everyday work. Still, you should try never to lose that main goal. That's why many nonprofits make their mission statement into a slogan. Repeat it several times, write it down, hang it on the wall, and always remember what you are doing this for. Losing that initial fame can be fatal for a nonprofit.

## Starting for Real

You have decided to create a nonprofit. The goal has been set; the mission statement is ready; you are already looking for a facility and researching how to hire people. However, creating an organization from scratch can already be a challenging process for someone who's used to it and a nightmare for someone who hasn't done anything like this before.

The first step is creating a business plan. Start with an overview of the entire operation, which should be included on the first page of the document. This should be short and powerful and work as an elevator pitch for your entire business plan. Many investors don't read past this summary, so make yours the best it can be to encourage them to turn the page.

It's also crucial to make a market analysis to get an idea of your competitors and the strengths, weaknesses, opportunities, and threats—also known as the SWOT analysis. This will help you have an overview of the chances of your organization succeeding.

The next step is to organize products and services, detailing what you plan to do and why you should be the one doing it. You should also include tangible products that are going to be produced, such as custom mugs, t-shirts, jewelry, and head caps that are going to bring money to the organization.

Next, you should do an operation plan that will contain the plans to set a physical space for the organization, the supplies you'll need, like stationery and furniture, for example. Then, how do you plan to offer your services and the profile of an ideal staff, including volunteers? You should also list each member of the staff and define their functions to make the best of their time and efforts.

At last, we have the financial plan, which is what most investors are interested in. If you don't have any notions of accounting, it's wise to hire professional help. This part of your report will be explaining how the money will be circulating within your nonprofit, how it will benefit the public and pay the staff, and how much of it you need to raise to achieve those goals.

Always have a clear idea of what kind of budget you need to fulfill the nonprofit's mission. Employees need to be paid, supplies must be bought, expenses have to be covered, and you will need to keep everything accounted for in order to maintain your 501(c)(3) status. That could mean hiring an accounting firm to take care of the paperwork—and that costs money.

Starting the budget of a nonprofit from scratch means not having passed numbers as a basis. Many people start this process hoping they will be getting a certain amount of donations, only to be disappointed later on. So while creating a fundraising plan, keep in mind that you might get much less than you want to. And since your company's whole revenue is based on donations, it's better to be prepared.

The first year can be the hardest, for you will be starting to understand how the company works and the challenges that the mission presents. It's always frustrating when you can't achieve all the goals you set for your nonprofit, but don't despair. You can use that knowledge to set up a more realistic budget plan.

Creating a detailed marketing plan is vital for an organization that will make its revenue from donations. People will not donate to your nonprofit if they don't know it exists. Even if they do, they will need to be convinced that your organization is worth donating to. Marketing doesn't mean only attracting people to collaborate with your organization: it's also about building their loyalty. A donor will be much more inclined to continue donating if they receive a letter showing how their contribution is making a difference in people's lives.

## Funding the Operation

Nonprofits make most of their revenue out of regular individual donors, fundraising, corporate sponsors, government grants, and fees for services and goods. Individual donors can collaborate once or become recurring donors. That means that they will offer seasonal donations that are debited automatically in their bank accounts or on a website such as Donorbox. These donations are reliable and convenient for both the donor and recipient and can be included in your annual budget.

Fundraising can include solicitations via phone calls, social media, email, and snail-mail. You can also do it in person at specific events and through advertising in the media. Many for-profit organizations include donations to charities in their budget and are glad to have their name and logo attached to a nonprofit that serves the needs of its community. You can also appeal to them to let you speak to their employees to get personal donations.

If you feel overwhelmed by this process, you can always hire a grant seeker. This is a professional with experience in finding the right grants and writing you a full proposal. You can find grant seekers online, and most of them work freelance. The best way of finding them is by putting an ad on a website such as LinkedIn. There are also volunteering websites where you can get a grant seeker for free—just be careful to hire someone who knows what they're doing!

Grants are not gifts! You'll have to prove to the grantor that you are using their money for the cause that's being rewarded. That's especially true with public grants since you'll be receiving taxpayer money. It's important to keep records of all expenses and transactions to prove that you are using the grant for the right purpose.

## Building Your Team

A company is only as good as its staff. So be careful while hiring the people you are going to be working with. They need to be aligned with the nonprofit's mission but also have to be competent, committed, and trustworthy.

### *Board of Directors*

The board of directors must have at least three members, according to the IRS specifications. Of course, you could have more, but it's always advisable that they are in an odd number to prevent tied votes. While it's not a rule, it's better that members are not from the same family to keep things impartial.

While hiring a board, give preference to people who have expertise in their area of work and who can bring that experience to the nonprofit. The board members are going to secure finances, hire people and make sure that the organization is following its bylaws. A good practice is to divide the board into three-thirds and distribute among them the financial-, management-, and community-based expertise.

Board members might have to work as volunteers and do some extra work until everything is set into place. Give them realistic expectations of what they are expected to do, so they won't question it later. Their skills should be in service of the nonprofit's mission, and they shouldn't be doing it for the money.

## *Executive Director*

After choosing your board members, find an executive director who will be taking charge of the daily operations to fulfill the nonprofit's vision. You should hire an executive director based on their management experience, communication and planning skills, and ability to lead.

When hiring an executive director, keep in mind the strengths and weaknesses of your nonprofit and how that person can help to improve on both. A nonprofit must work for an outside cause, and many external factors can affect it. So it's not just about the work you do in your office, but what happens outside it.

Having an executive director with an advanced degree is desirable, but familiarity with the demographic being served can be just as important. If, for example, your nonprofit aims to advance education in a poor neighborhood, hiring an executive director with a bachelor's degree who grew up in that neighborhood can be better than hiring an outsider with a doctoral degree. This will help the organization integrate with the community and help build confidence with its members.

The executive director is a paid employee, and you should add their salary to the annual budget. Starting small means that you might not afford the ideal executive director right at the start. Still, it could be worth it to cut costs elsewhere to hire a great executive director that will take your nonprofit to the next level.

## Officers and Staff

Officers are the people who command the staff of your nonprofit. It's their responsibility to implement the decisions made by the board of directors. The staff will be the people who make the nonprofit work day-to-day. Small nonprofits usually start with a small staff composed of volunteers. With time, they become larger and can hire and pay more people. Some organizations have dozens of volunteers, but one or two paid employees to coordinate them.

The treasurer is an officer responsible for keeping track of the expenses, paying bills, managing the fees, and taking care of the organization's funds. This job includes keeping track of the books that are presented annually to the IRS, so the company can keep its 501(c)(3) status.

The committee chair helps to execute the projects and manages the office activities, such as organizing meetings, writing minutes, and implementing the local bylaws. The job also includes facilitating the interaction of board members by keeping all of them informed of the organization's activities.

Nonprofits that operate online need communication managers to take care of their social media, to organize campaigns, write and send emails, manage websites, send greeting cards, and do public relations. It's wise to hire someone with a degree in communications and who is a heavy user of social media. This is a job that, most of the time, can be done online.

An events manager will take care of conferences, workshops, receptions, public fundraisings, and many monthly and yearly gatherings. In addition, they must contact public speakers, provide the participants with food and drinks, and prepare materials such as brochures and offer greeting gifts.

A fundraising manager is a professional that specializes in raising money from sponsors, fundraisings, and grants. For individual grants, a fundraising manager will go beyond what the grant seeker can do. They will be looking for opportunities for your nonprofit, network with potential donors, companies, and governing bodies in order to find the best partnerships for the organization.

The staff includes the people that work under these managers in specific fields. It also includes secretaries, cleaners, administrative assistants, drivers, and other workers who are needed in any company and may work full-time or part-time, being paid or volunteering.

# Hiring People

After determining the roles that need to be filled in your nonprofit, it's time to work on the recruitment process itself. For each role, you should have a defined idea of who the perfect candidate should be.

Nonprofit organizations must withhold federal income taxes from their employees' paychecks. This will make them eligible for the Federal Unemployment Tax Act (FUTA), a program that encourages states to pay those who are out of a job. This tax must be paid by the nonprofit, not the employee. Nonprofits also must pay for Federal Income Tax Withholding (FITW) and Social Security and Medicare taxes (FICA). If you pay more than $600 to an outside consultant, you need to report those payments with Form 1099 before the end of the calendar year. Similar forms might be required by state law.

The first thing you need to start hiring is the Employer Identification Number (EIN), which we have mentioned in a previous chapter. The EIN functions like a social security number for your nonprofit. With that number in hand, you can create a bank account in the name of your organization and hire people to work in it. You can apply for an EIN number by visiting the IRS website and filling the forms online. Alternatively, you can download the forms, fill them by hand, and mail them to the IRS office.

For a tax-exempt nonprofit, it's necessary to form the organization legally before applying for an EIN. That's because the tax exemption is revoked if you cannot provide the annual information return for three years in a row. Whether or not your organization isn't formed by the time you apply for an EIN, that three-year period will start to be counted when you receive your registration number.

## *The Hiring Process*

Hiring staff for a nonprofit is the same as for a for-profit. However, in case you're hiring a paid staff, you will need to determine how much money you'll be able to spend on salaries, the type of hiring, whether it's contract or salaried, and the benefits involved.

Make sure your nonprofit is registered in the required state programs, including worker's compensation and unemployment insurance. Also, always make sure that the people you're hiring are eligible for working in the U.S. These legalities should be solved before you start writing the recruitment ad.

The ad itself should include the general duties of the job, the benefits of taking it, the weekly time commitment required, the type of hiring, and the desired qualifications for the position.

Many nonprofits rely on recommendations from their personal and professional connections when selecting people for an interview. It's easier to ask for a recommendation from a friend or a former colleague than to post an ad and wait for resumes. Hiring a subpar candidate as a favor for someone you know is a red flag, though, and could damage your organization.

## Hiring Board Members

The first people you should think of hiring are your board members. They are usually unpaid, and if that's the case, include that information in your ad. Websites such as Board Net USA, Board Match, BoardSource.com, and The Bridgespan Group specialize in the recruitment of board members for nonprofits.

An ad for a board member job in a nonprofit should describe in detail the organization's vision and history and how you plan to implement your ideas. Follow that with an organizational chart and schedule of the board meetings—remember that board members aren't available 24/7.

After you select the best candidates, it's time for the job interview. While interviewing a potential board member, you should start by asking what they know about the organization and what makes them want to offer their time and services. Next, ask them what attributes make a great board member and if they have them.

Use the interview to find out what they know about fundraising since this is one of the biggest obligations of a board member. Do they have any in-depth experience with that? Would they be willing to be the voice of your organization and spend time in fundraising calls and events? What about going to a lunch where the goal is to ask the host to give a contribution to the cause?

Ask the prospect board members about their experience and contact list. Would they be willing to use the network that they built during the years for fundraising purposes? Or would they feel that's too intrusive? Again, try not to pressure them or make it seem that refusing to share their contacts will be a decisive negative point in the interview.

Board members should have some level of autonomy over their calendars. Ask them if they would be available for the required meetings and for social events and fundraisings. If the candidate is too busy for that, it will be hard for them to be the face of your organization.

Different questions may arise during the interview, so don't be afraid to ask them. It's advisable not to conduct the interview alone but surround yourself with other employees. After the interview, you can discuss your impressions of the candidate. That will lead to a more balanced decision at the time of hiring.

The selected board members should sign a board member contract that ensures they will act according to the organization's bylaws. The contract should also inform of any compensation they might receive—be aware that to pay a board member more than $600 a year, you must issue an IRS Form 1099 Misc.

Once your board members are hired, make sure that they are familiarized with the organization's mission, chart, schedule, and contact information of all the people working there. The best way of doing that is through one-on-one orientation, guiding them through everything they must know. If you have any orientation material, such as books and brochures, make sure that they have a copy they can take home.

Some organizations go the extra mile and host a reception to welcome their new board members. These receptions can be open to the public, in which case they should be announced on the organization's website, social media, and the local press. They are great for introducing the board members to the staff and the people benefited by the nonprofit.

## *Hiring A Staff*

The biggest difference between hiring board members and staff is that staff are usually paid jobs whose salary comes from the organization's revenue. Hiring a new staff member is not always the only solution. Gaps in the staff can be filled by promoting existing members. Creating such opportunities will improve the morale among the staff and can be less costly than recruiting new people.

In case you need to hire someone, be aware that posting a job ad will attract many people. Your candidates should be well informed about the job they're expected to perform, including time requirements, salary, benefits, and obligations. A nonprofit might not pay and a for-profit firm, but you can make the job more attractive by pointing out the flexibility and a sense of purpose that guides the firm.

Holding multiple interviews will help you know the candidate better to ask different questions and receive detailed answers. These meetings don't have to be all in person and can happen by phone or internet apps. You will create a connection with the candidates, a process that will help you pick the best one and save a lot of time later.

Resist the temptation of taking a risk because you need to fulfill a position on short notice. A great resume doesn't guarantee that the applicant will deliver a brilliant performance. Getting to know your candidates through multiple interviews will also prevent you from hiring someone whose attitude clashes with what the organization stands for. This is especially true for nonprofits, where the dedication to the mission is the important thing.

If the recruiter doesn't have experience with the interviewing process, it's easy to be biased in favor of a candidate who offered a good first impression. It's important to look for important information. That's why, like in the board member selection, it's important to have more than one interviewer present so that you can compare your notes and impressions.

A good exercise is to contradict that first impression: look for the good things in a candidate that seems weak and hesitant; and the negative things in a candidate that's confident and charismatic. That exercise will help you balance the bias of that first impression.

Take some time to talk to other nonprofits to see if they can offer you leads for candidates. Be careful if someone recommends an unqualified person because they're a friend or relative. Pay attention to the ones that are recommended because of their good service.

Take the time to confirm the information included in the applicant's resume. If a candidate says they have a degree, it's worth the effort to call that college and ask about it. Also, call their past jobs and check the dates informed in the resume. Sometimes a candidate won't blatantly lie about having worked or studied at a certain place, but they will bend reality to impress you. Finding out about that can tell a lot about an applicant's work ethic.

# Chapter 3:
# Starting a 501c3 Nonprofit

In this chapter, we'll be showing you how to build a brand in the early stages of the creation of a charitable organization. We'll also see the legal requirements to starting a 501(c)(3) nonprofit. There are several state and federal laws you should know before creating an organization.

Creating a nonprofit can be an extensive enterprise. The fees incorporation law and tax exemption vary widely from one state to the other, ranging from $25-150. Applying for tax exemption can cost from $275-600. In addition, you'll have to rent an office space, with all the expenses that one requires, not to mention the hiring and training costs of your staff—a staff that you'll have to pay. And don't forget paying for a website domain and building, marketing costs, etc.

If you are still in the early stages, getting public grants to start off may look impossible. You might get some donations from the community, but they are usually not enough to get a company off the ground.

One solution is to conduct an online crowdfunding. These have become popular in the last years, for they allow people to sell their ideas to contributors in exchange for a reward. If you are creating, for example, an organization that helps kids to practice sports, you could offer a jersey with the signature of all the kids as a reward to someone who contributes largely. Smaller contributions could be repaid with the name of the donor appearing in a plaque at the organization's office, together with the names of everyone who made a similar donation.

Crowdfunding is a solid way of getting an idea off the ground. It isn't enough to keep it going, though. After everything is set, you will have to rely on conventional grants and donations to make it work. And to do that, you need to have a name that will represent your nonprofit.

## Creating A Catchy Name

Naming your nonprofit is one of the trickiest parts of the job and one of the most important. The name is the first thing people will know about your organization, their first contact with your mission and values. Therefore, it must be clever and catchy, leaving people wanting to know more about your work. On the other hand, you shouldn't make it too long, and be sure that the name is easy to remember and pronounce.

The name of the nonprofit must sound good to the public and not just for you. Rather than sitting with pen and paper for hours trying to figure out a good name, brainstorm it with your team. This is a case where the help of an outsider, be it a family member or friend, can produce excellent results.

The name of the organization will attract workers and volunteers and will make you feel more secure about creating it. However, you'll also need to have the name figured out to file the necessary forms for incorporating and tax exemption. Because of that, some people rush to create a name they can use for immediate purposes, figuring they can change it later.

Changing the name of an organization isn't that easy, though. Not only does it involve a lot of paperwork, but it can also be a disaster marketing-wise. Recognition doesn't come quickly in the world of nonprofits, and sticking to a name will help you build trust in your brand. Unfortunately, a name switch can doom that hard work and get you back to square one.

You should think of renaming the nonprofit if you feel there's a disconnect between the name and the mission, for example, if the name refers to a location that you no longer attend, a person you no longer work with, or if it's dated somehow. It can also be necessary in case you find out about another organization whose name is too similar to yours.

Celebrities usually lend their names to a foundation they created, donating their credibility to the organization. For example, Whitaker Peace & Development Initiative was created by Hollywood actor Forest Whitaker to help impoverished communities across the globe. Soccer player Lionel Messi created the Leo Messi Foundation, through which he promotes health, education, and inclusivity through sports.

If you don't have a famous person to back you up, consider a descriptive name that gives some information about your mission right away. For example, when you hear the name of organizations such as Save the Whales, Feed the Children, and Teach for America, it's clear what they are advocating for and who they are. However, be careful not to be too descriptive, or you can undermine the organization's chance of expanding in the future. For example, naming your profit after your neighborhood could be a problem in case you grow large and start working in other places.

One powerful example of an organization's name is Keep a Child Alive, a nonprofit dedicated to helping people in poor regions of Africa. The name doesn't just convey the organization's mission. It also conveys its urgency. Who would refuse to keep a child alive?

Combining words to create a name is a good idea when done well. A classic example is Americorps, where you can understand the wordplay with little effort. Another example is WARwanda (Water Access Rwanda), whose name implies a war against the shortage of water in Africa. Just be careful not to create a confusing new word. Having to explain the meaning of your organization's name to everyone is counterproductive and awkward.

Abbreviations work well when they can create a new word, such as CUSO International, which stands for Canadian University Service Overseas. People are more likely to say and remember the acronym than the full name of the organization. For example,

Beyoncé Knowles' charitable foundation dedicated to mental health is called BeyGOOD. The adding of a simple Y associates the work of the foundation to the celebrity in charge of it.

Abbreviations don't always sound good, so be careful when using this option. An example is WJSFF, a foundation created by Will and Jada Smith, which, despite its good work, is hard to remember and pronounce.

After brainstorming a few names, select the ones that sound better. Then, read the names out loud. Ask other people to read them for you. Is this a name that can stand by your organization's work? Will you have to spell it for people to understand it? Be sure that the name hasn't already been used by a different organization and that the website domain related to it is available. Also, be careful with names that might sound good to you but that sound like pre-existing words from other languages—especially obscene ones!

Compile a shortlist of names and ask for the opinion of different people. See how that name sounds for those inside and outside the organization. Pay attention to their advice, even if they are telling you to drop a name you love. It's better to compromise now than later when the brand is known and the paperwork is filled out.

Once the nonprofit has a name, it's time to build your brand. First, hire a professional to create a logo for the organization. Unless you are a trained designer, don't do it yourself, no matter how much money that will save you. The logo should be simple and strong, something that people will recognize, and that will tell something about the nonprofit's mission and work.

## Becoming Exempt

Now that you have a business name and a board of directors define your legal structure as being a trust, a corporation, or an association. Trusts and associations offer their members little protection against liability and are not the most common choice for nonprofits. Corporations are more secure and are eligible for government grants, making them the best choice for a nonprofit's legal structure.

The first step to create a nonprofit is to file a business entity in your operating state. That entity is a LLC, sole proprietorship, partnership, or corporation, all of which can operate in the three categories: nonprofit, for-profit, or not-for-profit. The process to create a corporation is straightforward, and the forms are easy to understand.

After forming the entity, you have to apply for the tax-exempt status by filing a Form 1024 with your request for an EIN. Then, you can start your entity in one of those categories and convert it to a different one, although the process can be complicated.

Keep in mind that the paperwork you need to fill could vary from state to state. Some states, for example, require you to publish a note in a local newspaper regarding the creation of the nonprofit. You can find more about the laws where you live by contacting your local National Association of State Charity Officials (NASCO). The registration process requires you to inform:

- The name of your nonprofit

- Name and address of the registering agent (founder)

- Nonprofit address

- Names and addresses of the board members

- Statement of purpose to which your nonprofit will operate

Make sure that you have the required license and permits that will comply with federal, state, and local laws—for example, the right to operate a business at your office's address. The next step will be to apply for exemption of federal income tax with the IRS.

Creating a nonprofit doesn't automatically exempt your organization from the income tax. The IRS requires a series of proofs before granting you tax exemption, and they will monitor your organization even after granting you 501(c) (3) status.

IRS Publication 557, Tax-Exempt Status for Your Organization, dictates that you have to fill the online Form 1023 (or 1023-EZ if for a small organization) to apply for a 501(c)3 exempt charitable group. This form, also known as Application for Recognition of Tax Exemption, is supposed to offer the IRS knowledge about the structure of the organization, its purpose, and the programs it's going to implement. They also require the following documentation:

- The organization's EIN, identifying it as a taxpayer

- Articles of incorporation

- Organizing documents

- The organization's bylaws

- A description of your activities

- Financial information

Together with the 28-page long-form, you need to attach several documents, which can amount to over 100 pages. With this document, the IRS will be checking the strength of your organization's structure, its commitment to conduct the activities according to the mission, and if you're serious about operating as a 501(c)(3).

Most states will require you to have a Charitable Solicitations Registration before you can start receiving donations. A State Corporate Tax Exemption is also required in most states. Important exceptions include California and tax, where you must apply for charity purposes according to specific laws.

The process can be lengthy, ranging from 3 to 12 months, if you haven't done the research before submitting your request. The IRS might turn down your request in case you cannot offer the proper answers regarding your planning for this organization. It's not enough to have an idea and the desire to do good if you cannot set up and manage your budget.

A quicker alternative to that process is affiliating with a nonprofit that already has 501(c)(3) status. The best way of doing that is finding a sponsor with a similar mission to your company, although there are some nonprofits that are open to affiliations to companies in different areas.

After getting the 501(c)(3) status, you need to provide the IRS with an annual 990 form. Tax-exempt organizations must fill this form annually to prove that they've been complying with the IRS demands since the 501(c)(3) status was granted. The form must be submitted annually by the fifteenth day of the fifth month. Not delivering it could imply in the cancelation of tax exemption.

- Form 990 asks for eight basic items about your organization:
- EIN, also referred to as a Taxpayer Identification Number (TIN)
- Tax year
- Legal name and mailing address
- Any other names used by the organization
- Name and address of at least one principal officer
- Website address
- Confirmation that the annual gross receipts of the organization are $50,000 or less

The best way of keeping your 501(c)(3) status is to run a tight ship and make sure that you know everything that's always happening. Keeping records of finances is essential, but you should also have minutes for every meeting and ask for regular reports from the board members and staff about what's going on daily. Have a file with records of every grant you applied for, whether you got it, and copies of receipts for donations. Finally, keep up to date with the nonprofit regulations—they change all the time and might catch you off guard.

If your organization's gross receipts are less or equal to $50,000, you are entitled to form 990-N, which is submitted electronically, without having to fill any paper forms. Known as the 990 Postcard, the 990-N is a short form comprising eight questions, and it's much easier and quicker to fill.

In case your gross receipts are equal to or less than $200,000 or your assets amount to less than $500,000, you are eligible for Form 990 EZ. Being four pages long, this is a short version of Form 990, though more detailed than 990-N.

Remember that your organization's finances are open to the public and will be subjected to constant scrutiny. That means you cannot be caught off guard. Something like a License to Fundraise, for example, may sound like a mere formality. However, this is a document that allows you to solicit funds inside a specific jurisdiction. It's possible to fundraise without having one, but it's not advisable, and it could lead to serious trouble with the IRS.

## Lobbying and Politics

IRS publication 557 limits the amount that 501(c)(3) nonprofits can use to lobby the government. It doesn't forbid it, though. Nonprofits can remain tax-exempt if they only reserve an insubstantial amount of their budget for lobbying. In addition, nonprofits are forbidden to engage in political campaigns, be it to support or go against a candidate.

To determine if a lobbying activity can be considered substantial, the IRS considers factors such as how much time and money the nonprofit is dedicating to the lobbying compared to what's been spent in the company's mission. They may also require the nonprofit to fill Form 5768, Election/Revocation of Election by an Eligible Section 501(c)(3) Organization to Make Expenditures to Influence Legislation. This form serves to calculate how much money the company spends with its mission in proportion to the lobbying.

Other kinds of 501(c) don't have that same limitation. A teachers' retirement fund association for example, which falls under 501(c)(11), may participate in an electoral campaign if a candidate is advocating for teacher's rights, or a veteran's association 501(c)(23) that wants to lobby against a congressional representative who wants to push a law that benefits this demographic.

## Fundraising

Since donations are the foundation of the organization's finances, pay special attention to fundraising. That is the act of requesting a contribution from donors, whether they are private, corporate, or foundations.

There are several different ways you can fundraise. Using over one will lead to better results. The most basic way is to call people on the phone or approach them on the street and tell them about your cause. While this often works, most people might find this method intrusive, which leaves a bad impression on your organization.

You can also solicit money through snail mail, social media, and emails. Crowdfunding websites are also helpful to raise money for a particular project. For example, if your company's mission involves restoring a house that's been destroyed by a natural incident, you can start a campaign to raise money for that.

While writing an email to ask for a donation, try to be brief and direct. Split the text into subject lines to make it more readable and try to get the reader's attention before requesting the donation. People receive several emails every day, and a message that asks for money right off the bat will end up in the spam folder. Your best chance is to write good content that will catch their attention and to also mention at the bottom that they can make a difference.

A key aspect of fundraising is storytelling. Asking someone to help children in need sounds vague while picking a specific child with a name and telling their story is much more powerful. Try not to exploit the situation of people, even if your intention is to help them, but make sure that the potential donor feels for that human being who's in need and who they can help with their donation.

The donors should feel that the story you're telling is about them. Make good use of the second person: you, your, yours. That will make them feel like an important part of that story. Hook the donor from the beginning, informing them of the difference they can make. Don't manipulate them to offer more than they can. Even if their first contribution is small, it's only the first of many.

Look at your donors not only as contributors but also as partners. People donate money to charities because they want to see things change, and you are the vehicle that makes that change happen. With that idea in mind, you can create a connection with your donors and earn their trust.

Keep an eye on the donor's retention rate. If they are donating less or nothing at all, a friendly call from the nonprofit's owner is a good idea. Talk to them, find out how they relate to your cause, and if there's anything you could do for them. Make the call personal and let them know how crucial their donation is.

You can also use social media to enhance your campaign's visibility. A peer-to-peer campaign is a model in which several individuals will create their own fundraising pages advocating for your cause. Then, they share this campaign with their contacts, spreading the word without extra cost to you.

Advertising on social media offers you access to a plethora of different individuals who could be interested in helping with your cause. In addition, investing money in a Facebook ad will get a post much more views than it would on its own. That works well if you have a Donate Now button on your Facebook page.

Nonprofits are entitled to government grants that aren't accessible to private parties. These grants can be local, state, and nation government based. Websites such as Grants.gov offer an overview of opportunities, so you can pick the one that better fits your needs.

Before starting the fundraising:

1.  Define your budget based on what you plan to accomplish.
2.  Do all the research you need to figure out the exact amount you need and how it's going to be used.
3.  Resist the temptation of creating a round number on top of your head.

Being lazy now can lead to judicial problems from donors who aren't pleased with how you spent their money.

A core number is the precise amount of money that you will need to offer a unit of service, which is a measure of service volume over a period. For example, a unit of service could be a school kit composed of the material a child needs to go through a school semester.

Create a sheet with the total expenses you have in a year, divided by the unit of services that you've offered or plan to offer. Having that number set will make things easier, allowing you to understand how much of a difference each donation will make. For example, knowing that $10 is enough to buy a school kit for a child means that a $50 donation will attend five kids.

It's not just for projects: you should know how each cent that you get will help you to maintain your organization. That includes your facilities, marketing material, human resources, and equipment. Your donors will be more inclined to help you if they know precisely where their money is going to be used.

With the core number in mind, you can put together a gift range chart, which will help you visualize your campaign goals. This chart makes it easier to create your fundraising strategy, knowing how much you should ask from each donor, which areas to focus your campaign, and see whether your campaign is being successful. With those numbers in mind, it's time to figure out who your donors should be. Depending on your mission, you should find people that are sympathetic and willing to help. If you are promoting gender equality, for example, most of your donors will probably be women. That doesn't mean that men won't help, only that you should pay specific attention to the female demographic.

Try to get partnerships with companies that operate in your community, such as small shops, restaurants, and clinics. Having your name attached to a business that people know and trust can be a golden opportunity for your nonprofit.

Whatever approach you use, always send a thank-you message to the donors after they make their contribution. Keep them in your email list and send them a greeting card on their birthdays and on the holidays. That will keep you in their minds, so the next time they think of donating money to charity, your organization will be the first they'll think about.

## Standard Operating Procedures

Nonprofits can use the standard operating procedure (SOP) to define the expected. SOPs allow you to complete the daily tasks according to regulation, including your bylaws. If two chapters of the same nonprofit, in different continents, follow the same SOP, they will provide a similar service.

SOPs are crucial for nonprofits, for it's by following them that members of the staff make sure they are acting according to the budget. For example, if an organization's SOP stipulates that its members must do a task in a certain way and in a certain amount of time, it makes it easier to identify the core number of that task. It also improves the efficiency of the staff, raising the quality of their efforts.

The mission of your nonprofit should be the first goal of the SOP, but it can also be about minor tasks that one or two employees must follow. Next, you should outline the steps to achieve that goal, as well as the problems you might find on the way. After defining these issues, figure out the means and procedures that each member must engage in.

Following a SOP is a guarantee you won't have to improvise in case of an eventuality. For example, suppose one of your workers calls in sick the day of a big presentation. In that case, you won't have to despair trying to find a solution because you already have a code that instructs how to redistribute the staff or call a volunteer who's available that day. Likewise, if a donor stops giving, you have written everything you need to say when you call them.

This process is useful not only to increase your productivity and optimize your time but also helps to keep accountability on everything that's happening in your organization. That will be crucial when we analyze filing audit reports.

# Chapter 4:
# Raising Awareness and Support

There's no point in creating a great nonprofit with a solid mission and a dedicated staff if people don't know you exist. The concept of nonprofit involves working together with a community to achieve results. So you need to raise awareness among that community, and with people outside of it, since most of your revenue will be earned from donations.

Turn your nonprofit into a brand. As we've seen, you need to have a catchy name, a logo, and a mission statement. People need to associate your brand with the work you do and know you're trustworthy.

You need to have a website that's going to function as your organization's headquarters, a web address which people will see first when they type the name of your organization on Google.

## Your Official Website

Visiting a website is an experience. If the experience is positive, people will want to come back looking for updates. A negative experience will give the opposite result. Unless you are a trained web designer, you shouldn't try to build the page by yourself from scratch. Having the help of an experienced professional will make a difference. You can also try a membership website builder that offers straightforward systems for people to drag and drop their content.

A website is supposed to answer all the questions that the visitor has regarding your nonprofit. Therefore, it has to be attractive to look at but also easy to navigate and load fast. That will lead the visitor to engage with your mission and decide whether they want to donate or volunteer.

The first thing your visitors will see is a homepage, which should work as a pitch. Include an impacting picture, your logo, and a phrase that summons up how important your work is. Some websites include donation buttons at their homepage but never put them before the mission statement, or that will sound like e-begging.

Your website should have a section entitled About Us, where you are going to tell the visitor about how the organization was founded and have photos and short bios of its members. These mini bios should be fun and easy to read, and you can include details such as the member's hobbies and pets.

Visitors will want to know about your nonprofit's past work. They will want to integrate with your organization if you can show your successful work. If you're just starting out, you can include your future goals on the website and offer concrete details of how you plan to achieve them. Include pictures of the nonprofits facilities and the people you want to assist, but resist the temptation of being melodramatic by, for example, including pictures of starving children to get more clicks.

When you tell the story of your nonprofit, make the person reading it feel like they're part of the story. Create a narrative where donors play a strong part and make them feel how crucial their help is to the organization's success. Knowing that they can help change the lives of people will encourage them to get involved and contribute.

Having a blog with regular posts about relevant issues will bring people from many backgrounds, which can be converted into donors and volunteers. For example, suppose you have a nonprofit that helps amputees. In that case, you can create a blog where you post regular news about that subject, as well as detailed information about prosthesis and inspirational stories about the people you assist.

Donating should be easy, allowing people to make their contribution with a few clicks and without printing any materials. The best way of doing it is by having a donation button that the visitor can click on and fill a form with their payment details. The donate button should be present on every page of your website, so the visitors can click on it while they're reading your material.

The visitor should have the alternative of making single donations recurring payments that will be charged automatically on their credit card every month. Set up a system in which the donor will be reminded at least a couple of days before the automatic payment.

Each campaign should have its unique form, allowing people to know what they are donating for. The form should be simple to fill, asking only the most important questions. The form should also inform the different giving levels, not only regarding how much money is being donated but the different benefits of each amount.

Donors will want to know how their money will be used. When asking for donations, be clear about how they are going to be used. Some nonprofits set milestones they need to achieve to conduct an activity. For example, if your nonprofit provides clean water to a community, you can establish on your website how much money you need to drill a well. You can also use your blog to post news about how those donations are benefiting the community. Remember: you need to engage people before asking them for money, and the best way of doing that is reassuring the importance of what you're doing.

If you want to offer your visitors a different option than donating money, your website should have a page entitled More Ways to Give. For example, you can get donations of clothes, books, toys, and food, gather volunteers to work online or in-person and offer all sorts of help that doesn't require informing their credit card numbers.

Another thing that should be simple is the Join Us form the visitors must fill to associate with the organization. This form should be online—no printing materials—and the members who sign in should be granted special features, such as newsletters and access to the Members Only area of the website. In this area, they should have access to a calendar with all the upcoming events and the steps to join them.

Web volunteering is a growing trend. If you have a job that a volunteer could do from his home computer, you have a pool of volunteers from all over the world. People apply for volunteering jobs to gather work experience and to help people in places they've never been to. Use this diversity in your favor, hiring volunteers from different backgrounds and cultural experiences.

People are going to access your website from many devices. So your web designer should be able to create versions of it that are accessible on mobile devices such as smartphones and tablets. Studies show that 60% of visitors come from mobile devices, a demographic that could make a lot of difference with donations.

It's never a bad idea to have your content accessible to people with disabilities. An accessible website should also be keyboard-friendly, working without the help of a mouse. Other features include:

- Caption text in videos for people with hearing impairment.
- Links with descriptive texts.
- Images with alt tags for people with sight impairments.

Choosing the colors of your text and background can also make it more readable—no blue fonts over purple backgrounds—and the text should be easily resizable without breaking the text.

## Other Ways of Gathering Donors

Creating local awareness can be as simple as sending a press release to a local paper, hosting receptions at your office, and distributing brochures and other promotional items. Brochures might sound old-fashioned in the digital age, but having printed material circulating will help raise awareness of your organization.

Press releases are documents used to ask the press to do a story about a subject. Newsrooms are flooded with dozens of press releases every day, both print and electronic, and have to select the ones that look promising.

Sending press releases won't guarantee that the vehicle will be making a story about you. Still, you should send it to all the relevant vehicles, being careful not to mix up the name of the reporter you're contacting. You will find the template of a press release at the end of this book.

If you are hosting a social event, send the release a few days before, preferably a week. You can have events such as a luncheon, a picnic, or even an afternoon of games to break the ice. If your nonprofit deals with children, you can ask them to do presentations during the event. For example, a nonprofit that helps children's education can ask the students to read a poem they wrote for the guests.

Such events are significant to strengthen the bonds with the donors. They also help to gather new people who have never heard of your cause. That works especially well if you're hosting a lecture or workshop. People will attend these because of the content being presented and will go back home knowing about your cause.

There are professional public speakers for hire, but you can always step in front of the microphone and say some words about your mission. You can also find people who will do that work eventually, so they can promote their own product to the people attending.

It's useful to talk about a historical or scientific matter that relates to your nonprofit, even if tangentially, rather than reciting the same material people can find in a brochure. That's the same principle as content marketing, which consists in creating content that isn't direct promotion, but that builds your image as an expert in a certain field. By doing this, you will be offering knowledge for donations. And don't forget to offer a certificate of attendance at the end of the lecture.

Talk to people on your staff, and you might find out that they have private interests that could be turned into interesting lectures. Maybe your secretary has a collection of old postcards, or the finance director knows everything about James Bond movies. Even if it's something that's not directly connected with the work you're doing, it could be a way of attracting new people. Whether you're turning this into lectures or blog posts, this is a powerful tool.

Whatever social events you are hosting, it's crucial to have someone photograph and record the material to share on social media. Ask people if you can use their images before posting these online. Add fun and informative descriptions to these posts, so people who missed the event will feel like coming to the next one.

If you don't have the funds to host a reception, you can involve people in community service. It's great for furthering the cause, doing good, and engaging people in a friendly environment. An organization that advocates for the well-being of the elderly can gather young people to visit retirement homes and make presentations for the old-timers there. Always have a photographer registering these moments, as they make for valuable marketing material.

## The Importance of Social Media

Social media is a useful resource to engage with people. A well-done social media campaign can connect you with the right people and interact with them with minimal cost. It's also a way of having people constantly talking about your nonprofit's mission to their own followers.

People's attention span is lower now than it was ten years ago, mostly because the internet can be accessed everywhere, on a plethora of devices. Because of that, it's hard to get a message across before something else steals your viewer's curiosity. Thus, the ideal is to have an internet presence across several platforms.

First, figure out what platform better fits your needs. The key ones are Facebook, LinkedIn, and Twitter for their usability and number of members. They are also quickly recognizable, even for people who don't have accounts in them.

You can create a Facebook page for your nonprofit through your personal account. You will add the name of your page and select the category of nonprofit. Use the logo of your organization as the page's avatar. The cover picture should be something attractive that speaks of your work, for example, a picture of the people whose lives you plan to impact.

From there, you need to gather followers. The first step is to ask your Facebook contacts to like your page—there's a special button for that. Next, it's important to keep posting regularly, or else people will forget you. Tools such as Buffer and Hootsuite allow you to program your content, which will be posted automatically without you having to be online.

While you can post almost any subject on your Facebook page, LinkedIn is a social media dedicated only to business. Therefore, your posts should follow that theme. Setting up a page on LinkedIn is a simple process. They will ask about your company's type and size, as well as your contact information. Your header section should also include a tagline and a button with a link to your website.

You can add your phone number and full address, as well as relevant hashtags and languages used in the organization. Some of these fields are optional, and you can launch your page without filling them. Having a fully filled page will help you get more views, though, and you should take the time to complete it.

The appeal of Twitter is an open space that gives a voice to people and organizations. The most important issues of each day are highlighted, breaking news appears there before anywhere else, and powerful people such as celebrities, influencers, and politicians have a direct link with their followers.

Having your nonprofit on Twitter will provide you that direct link with your donors, staff, and beneficiaries, as well as other organizations. Many audiences use Twitter, and you can build lasting relationships that will impact your work. But be careful with what you post: people have jeopardized their entire careers because of a thoughtless tweet. When you wonder if your post will offend the wrong people, it's better not to tweet it.

## Software Systems

The software that you use in your organization is going to dictate the rhythm of your work, so do the proper research before picking one. Changing a software system takes a lot of effort, not only to transfer the data but also to train your staff to use the new one.

Software can do administrative work that doesn't require human hands. For example, you can use them to manage your membership database, register new members, receive payments, and collect donations.

Having multiple softwares will give you more autonomy to change to a different one later on. Have separate training sessions for each one, though. Without integration between the systems, it gets harder to exchange data between them.

Multiple software can be attractive for nonprofits with a limited budget, for they usually offer a free option for low use. You can start with this option, but if your nonprofit grows, you might have to upgrade your plans to these software. In addition, using multiple options means that you have to monitor the cost of each one.

The most used software are:

- Email providers
    - Gmail, Outlook, ProtonMail, etc.
- Donation providers
    - DonorPerfect, Qgiv, etc.
- Microsoft Word Online
- Microsoft Excel Online
- Eventbrite (event organizer)
- QuickBooks (basic accounting)
- PayPal (payment collector)
- WordPress (website management)

The software in this list will take care of the basic needs of a nonprofit organization. If you want to have a more robust and integrated system, investigate membership management software. It can include a series of features that provide all the services you need, which will be intertwined in the same system.

The costs of running a membership management software are lower in the long run. You can have a system that's designed for the needs of a nonprofit, something that the list above doesn't offer. The membership management software also makes it easier for you to train new staff, and it's also faster to switch to a different system. On the other hand, you might have some trouble integrating your membership management software with new software. For example, if you discover a new program that helps you with a specific part of your finances, you might have some trouble using it together with the membership management software.

The cost of your membership could grow together with your nonprofit. Familiarize yourself with the pricing structure of the software to avoid headaches. For example, some providers charge fees for setting up the system and providing support for training. Include those costs in your monthly and annual budget.

An online system should be intuitive and easy to use. Having an overly complicated system can doom your entire enterprise. On the other hand, a good system will improve the workflow of your staff and match you with the best donors and volunteers. Multiple software and membership management software both have their pros and cons, so make sure you understand them before picking one.

# Chapter 5:
# Managing Finances

The 501(c)(3) status is a fragile thing, and you must be extra careful in order to keep it. The IRS keeps a special eye on the restricted gifts and whether you have misspent the funds you got from your donor.

Each implemented program needs special care. You should pay attention to how much they cost, what results they brought, how hard it was to fundraise and to implement the program, and what can be learned and improved in future ones. Ask yourself how likely it would be that donors will continue to collaborate and what can be done to improve that. Sometimes, the program you're most attached to has to be cut out when you close the month.

When presenting the monthly results for your board of members, make a presentation with dashboards that include graphics and images. Bar and pizza charts, illustrations, and organization charts will display the pertinent data and make it easier for the board to understand. You might have board members who don't have any financial training, so this can make things as easy as possible for them.

Make use of the human factor. Create a simple narrative that will give context to the numbers. Let them know how many people were helped, how many new donors you got, and the units of service that were implemented. You should aim to become bigger, but also better. Improving the quality of service is as crucial as extending that help to more people.

While you should use most of your money in your programs, it's wise to open a reserve fund. Estimate a percentage of donations that can go into that fund, and don't touch it unless your nonprofit is facing financial distress. Since your financial records are open to the public, you should be transparent about them. Funders wouldn't like to know that their money is going to a secret fund.

A reserve could also be useful to help fund future projects with the revenue of your current fundraising. For example, if you need $1,000 for a project but end up getting double that, you can put aside part of that money and use it in the next project. Sure, the extra money could make the current project even better, but since you can't pocket anything that's not spent, why not use it for the nonprofit's next enterprise— always being transparent to your collaborators.

A tool that enables you to estimate your future financial situation is the cash flow forecast. This is a spreadsheet where you will be able to see your expected payments, receivables, and future expenses. This way, you will know your financial situation at any time and understand how much you should have in the reserve funds.

# The Essence of Financial Services

You should keep a good accounting system and keep your basic records always up-to-date. In addition, you should do monthly reconciliation at least once a month, matching the balance of your accounts records with a statement of the bank in which you have a cash account.

A nonprofit should also have a statement of cash flow, which is the same that a nonprofit should have. This statement is a report of how much cash and equivalents enter and leave the company every month. It also includes the investments made at how much money was used to purchase long-term assets.

If all that sounds too complicated, start by keeping a file or reference system that's constantly updated. That will make your life easier when you must find an important document. All aspects of your nonprofit finances should be well-established and documented in this system. That includes the use of the funds, the authorization of purchases, and the act of paying your employees. If you must ask someone to cross the street and buy a pencil, that should be accounted for.

Financial management is the backbone of the entire organization. Without it, programs can't happen, staff can't get compensated, and the mission can't be fulfilled. It's easy to think that in a small organization, one person should have the responsibility of maintaining the books and records. But you should make it a policy that every employee, including volunteers, should cooperate in this effort.

Your organization will need to produce an annual statutory account representing your financial activity during that year. The finance department should start preparing these months ahead by preparing and filing the documents in the correct system. Here, too, it's a good idea to use a narrative while presenting your annual activity to a member of the IRS. That will give them an idea of your nonprofit's mission and how those finances are being used to fulfill it.

Having both hard and digital files is useful to check any discrepancy that may arise. When you file a donation, have the donor fill a form with their contact details, home address, and social security number.

## Form 990

Public trust makes nonprofits work. People see them as organizations dedicated to do good and give them the benefit of not paying taxes, as well as receiving their donations. Finding out that a nonprofit is abusing that trust will impact not only the people involved but the whole sector.

You will be getting donations from people and corporations who identified with your cause. The only thing they ask in return, apart from the tax exemption, is that your organization fulfills that cause. For example, you can't use the money you raised to buy clothes for the homeless and use it to fix your computer unless that computer plays a part in fulfilling that mission.

Not disclosing your financial information can catch the attention of the IRS and lead to audits. Your tax exemption status is subject to your transparency and accountability. You are required to provide a high level of financial oversight, and since these finances are public, watchdog groups are inclined to go digging into it to find irregularities.

Tax-exempt organizations are required to submit Form 990, offering an overview of their activities and governance, as well as other financial information. The deadline to submit this form is May 15 of the tax year calendar, or on the fifteenth day of the fifth month after the fiscal year. For every late filing, there's a $20 penalty.

Forgetting to file the 990 forms for three consecutive years could cause you to lose your tax-exempt status. If your form isn't in accord with the IRS requirements, you could be asked to resubmit it. It saves time to get it right the first time. There is filing software that can track your 990 records and help you file for your return.

To fill out Form 990, you will first have to go through internal and audited financial statements. The internal statement is created inside by the organization, with the help of a bookkeeper, and is written to help understand the organization's industry. It also serves as a preparation of the audited financial statement.

The financial audit statement is audited by an independent certified public accountant (CPA) who will check the data provided by visiting the nonprofit site, interviewing members of the staff and the community, talking to the donors, and conducting other analytical procedures. Then, the CPA is going to report on whether the information in the report is true.

The board members handle both reports and for the information provided on File 990. If you are in doubt about how to proceed with these reports, don't do it by yourself. A mistake could be fatal for your organization. Getting the help of an accountant or an auditor is the best investment you can make in this situation.

The IRS provides a filing program created specifically for Form 990. Using this e-filer improves your chance of submitting the form without mistakes. In addition, this software will send you a message to let you know when it's time to file your form. It is free to use for organizations with a receipt of less than $100,000, and it provides special state forms for Hawaii, Michigan, and New York.

The first time you use it, the e-filer uses your nonprofit's EIN to pull your tax information for the IRS database. This information is safely stored using a bank-level security system. Next, the e-filer will ask you a series of questions that they will use to fill your form. You will see the details of your tax filings by each chapter of your nonprofit and visualize them separately.

Not submitting the 990 Form on time will incur a $20 fine per day. In addition, failing to submit this form for three consecutive years will cause the revocation of your tax-exempt status at the filing due date of the third year. States can also prevent a nonprofit from receiving grants and large donations if they don't deliver the form on time. The maximum penalty could reach $10,000 or 5% of the organization's gross receipts, whatever is less. For example, if it's proven that your nonprofit makes more than $1,000,000 in gross receipts, you could be penalized $100 per day with a maximum charge of $50,000.

In case you cannot file your form in time, you can gain some time by submitting Form 8868. An exempt organization can request an automatic three-month extension to file its return. They can also apply for a three-month extension on that extension if they feel there hasn't been enough time.

The IRS imposes strict control requirements over nonprofits. For example, it's important that all the money that comes and goes into a nonprofit must be traceable. With that, the IRS prevents the tax-exemption system from being abused.

Since all the profit earned by the organization is supposed to be reabsorbed and used to fulfill its mission, the accounting should be tight and inform where each penny is going. A mistake—whether an honest slip or an intentional fraud—will be easily spotted, and you'll have to explain yourself to the IRS. In this situation, it helps to have an experienced accountant by your side.

Keeping your bookkeeping and accounting up to date is crucial while running a nonprofit. Some organizations have a bookkeeper or accountant in their staff, but outsourcing this service is a more affordable alternative. Accounting offices will have a team of professionals with the proper education and experience to conduct this activity. If possible, hire one that specializes in working with nonprofits, for they can offer personalized services.

You can do basic accounting with the aid of a spreadsheet. Start by comparing your budget with your monthly revenue and expenses. Remember that budgets are documents that plan your financial needs for the future, unlike a financial statement which reports your past transactions. Then calculate the difference it will make at the end of the year. Those numbers will show you what kind of accountant you should look for.

The tax code for nonprofits is extremely difficult, making the tax reporting much more complicated than for nonprofits. Be careful if a volunteer offers to do your accounting. Ask about their school and professional history. While their intentions may be good, it can lead to a lot of trouble if they're not prepared to do the job. If your car broke down on the road, would you rather wait for a mechanic or ask the first person who passes by to fix your engine?

While briefing your board members, inform them of all the different ways your tax report could go wrong. They should know how crucial financial transparency is. Otherwise, they could jeopardize the organization by accepting an extravagant gift or using the organization's resources to generate unrelated profit.

As an organization that survives out of grants and donations, you should know the different programs created by organizations and the government. Many websites online offer an updated list of new grants, with their requirements and benefits.

You should also be up to date with news, both local and national, to find out about new opportunities. Of course, following politics is important, but you can also get useful information from unlikely places. For example, a famous actor who was involved in a car accident creates a grant to raise awareness of the dangers of drinking and driving.

## Important Metrics

It's also useful to track other metrics, such as restricted versus unrestricted net assets. Restricted net assets are those donations that are done for a specific purpose. For example, if you get grant money to be used to buy medicines, you can't use it to pay the rent of your office. Unrestricted assets have no strings attached; you get that money and use it as you see fit for your nonprofit.

The biggest violation a nonprofit can make is misspending the money from a donation, which can only happen with restricted gifts. It can be a problem if the donor is not aware of the differences between these two types of donations. A simple solution would be to provide a disclaimer while asking for a donation to clarify that their money can be used for several different purposes. If you must use restricted funds for other activities, contact the donor and ask for permission to repurpose their gift.

In order to comply with the type of grant you're applying for, understand its requirements. Then, the design of your application should be directed to those requirements. Don't apply for a grant that doesn't fit your needs because you think you have a good chance of passing it. This could incur several penalties in the future.

Any asset in your nonprofit, be it your office, a program, or a stapler, must have its lifespan determined so you can calculate its depreciation. This is a way of calculating the use of that item until it has lost its value. Some items suffer depreciation, while others don't. You should create a schedule to know when you can use that item and when it will be necessary to replace it with a new one.

If your nonprofit doesn't have a fixed stream of income, you will always be at risk of running out of money. A statement of financial position is going to provide an idea of the organization's finances. Make a list of your assets in the order of liquidity and how fast you can convert them into money. You should also list your liabilities in order of their length of obligation.

## *Statement of Activities*

A statement of activities is the nonprofit equivalent to an income statement. While nonprofits use the income statement to report their financial results, a nonprofit will use the statement of activities to quantify its revenue and expenses in a specific period. You can create a simple spreadsheet with two rows or create a more complex one. That spreadsheet should include items such as:

- Member dues
- Contributions
- Fundraising events
- Program fees
- Gain on sale of investments
- Investment income
- Grants

Your statement of activities should include your program expenses. This will allow you to see how much each program cost, how well the money was spent, and if you can afford to continue it. For example, a support services expense will provide a snapshot of how well the organization is working and the changes that might need to be made.

Income such as donation of equipment, food, clothes, and anything that isn't cash, must go into the revenue column of your statement of activity. If you had any expense related to those donations, such as paying to install a donated printer, record that in your expense column.

Some donations might fit into the generally accepted accounting principles (GAAP). That would be, for example, if a client who's an artist would donate a painting for you to hang in your office. This is considered a gift but isn't turned into cash, and therefore can't be classified as either an expense or revenue.

## *Statement of Functional Expenses*

This is a list where you can organize the expenses of your nonprofit, whether they are related to administrative activities, fundraising, or implementing programs. These functions are divided into types of expenses, such as rent, transportation, and salary.

The people who examine this document should have a clear idea of how your nonprofit balances the funding and expenses and whether it's able to maintain its activities. This balance means being able to run a solid enterprise, maintaining the quality of your projects with a competent staff. If your finances are out of proportion, that could call the attention of the IRS.

## *Statement of Cash Flow*

This statement will inform the idea that's coming in and out of your organization. That should be calculated in a specific amount of time, be it a year, a month, or a more specific period. This statement includes three sections:

- Operating activities: funds raised from grants and donations or by offering a service.

- Investing activities: expenses from purchasing a vehicle or piece of equipment or from long-term investing.

- Financing activities: money earned from issuing or redeeming bonds.

## *Annual Statutory Report*

We've already discussed at length the importance of Form 990 and how you should use it to provide the IRS an annual report of your financial activities. Still, we will talk a little more about the process of writing this document.

Annual reports must be made as the year goes by. Leaving it for the last minute can be disastrous. Even if you have the files all in your system, ready to be pulled and examined, it will be a herculean effort to go through all of them and write the data you need.

A much more practical way is to add data to your report as that data is collected. This must be done daily, and it's like building a house brick by brick. When the time comes for you to present your report, you'll be impressed by how big that house has become.

The data you'll need includes your organization's:

- Employer Identification Number (EIN)
- Legal name
- Tax year
- Website
- Gross receipts

Keep the report simple and offer an interesting narrative, rather than throwing numbers at the page. This narrative must show the auditor the impact that your nonprofit is having in your community. This will help them see how you comply with their requirements, and it'll help you keep your 501(c)(3) status.

Once submitted, Form 990 becomes public information, accessible to any taxpayer. That means you don't have to keep files of your past years' forms: you can access them. Still, the IRS recommends you keep records for at least three to seven years after the date you filed the return. You can track your records by using a filing software. Enter your EIN number, and the software will pull your information from the IRS database.

You should always be able to provide copies of your three most recently filed annual inform returns, together with a copy of your application for tax exemption. This includes schedules, attachments, and any relevant supporting documentation. Some nonprofits choose to save time by having these documents available from a link on their website.

## *Audits*

Because of their tax-exempt status, nonprofits are subject to harsher audit requirements. In addition, their level of transparency must be above average since their finances are open to the public, and they have to account for their mission.

The IRS might require your nonprofit to conduct an independent audit. This happens when an independent audit firm conducts an examination on your records to check your financial statements, transactions, accounting practice, and internal control.

All processes must be established and accounted for. Having a good filing system will make your life easier. Keep every authorization of purchase and specific documents every time the organization purchases a product or service. This should be a policy of the organization, and every member of the board and staff should help with it.

## Managing Your Money

Having settled your core number, you should know how much it takes to promote each activity. You should also have an idea of how much it costs to raise the money that flows into your nonprofits. Not only in terms of donations and programs but also the cost of rent, paying your staff, and recurring bills. Having these numbers in mind will make it harder for you to be surprised by a shortage of money.

Use financial dashboards while presenting your budget to your board. Some of them might not have the required business training, yet it's crucial that they understand the situation of the organization well. These dashboards shouldn't be limited to money-related issues. Include the people your nonprofit helped, how their lives were changed, the level of interest of the volunteer, and how those numbers related to previous years.

Managing money isn't always about finding the cheapest solutions. Sometimes you must invest a little more cash into an item or service that's going to last longer. For example, if you buy cheap shelves for your office, you will have to change them periodically.

That means removing all the items before removing them, screwing the new shelves on, and putting everything back. But, of course, that is if the shelves don't break and throw your stuff in the ground before you change them.

The same goes, for example, for your website. Everyone seems to know someone who's good at computers and who'll create your page for a lower price than a professional designer. But, unfortunately, that could turn into a nightmare later, and you'll have to spend more money to hire the professional who should have done the work in the first place.

The services you offer your community should be as good as the budget allows. Your core number shouldn't be the lowest denominator possible, but instead, it should allow you to provide good services. You might have to decide whether you are going to help more people with less quality or focus your attention on a smaller group so you can give them better treatment.

Finding an equilibrium between these two options is tough but necessary. Your resources are limited, and it's better to manage that problem than to deny it. On the other hand, the fact that your organization depends on donations makes your options limited, and from time to time, you'll have to make tough decisions to get reasonable results and still be able to keep your tax-exempt status.

## Local Laws

Depending on the state your organization is based on, you might be required to file one or more reports per year. The filing requirements are financial reports, corporate filings, state tax-exemption filings, and fundraising registrations. They might also require a renewal of your initial registration and signatures of corporate officers.

These requirements can vary, and it's a good idea to familiarize yourself with the laws of your state's government agency. This information should be displayed on their official website, including updates on recent changes and templates of the required forms. Most states do the entire process online now.

You might also have to file a form to cancel the registration of your nonprofit in a state where it's no longer operating. This means filling more paperwork, together with the required fees. If you move to another state without doing this process, it could cause problems with your tax-exempt status.

## Conflicts of Interest

Conflicts of interest arise when one or more board members can't be impartial to the organization. In addition, members of the board shouldn't have personal or financial benefits from their position. For example, if the nonprofit creates a program to promote sports, and one of the board members owns a sports equipment store, they should be kept away from decisions that involve buying such equipment.

The IRS requires that nonprofit organizations have a written policy regarding conflict of interest, which should be included in Form 990. This policy needs to establish the board's rules to identify and manage such conflicts. Its primary goal is to prevent board members with conflicts of interest from participating in the organization's activities.

Anyone who believes they have a conflict of interest should report themselves to the board. That will work in the best interest of the organization if done in good faith. However, if the board member decides not to inform his fellows about the conflict of interest, that could incur an excess benefit transaction.

The excess benefit transaction happens when a disqualified person gets an economic benefit from an organization. Any person who has substantial influence over a tax-exempt organization, whether they exercise it, is considered a disqualified person. Most officers of an organization, including the president and the board members, fall under that title. In addition, any person who took part in the organization's foundation, has authority over its budget and revenue, or manages a substantial segment of the organization can also be considered disqualified personnel.

If the sports equipment store we mentioned gets a contract with the nonprofit, not because of the quality of their merchandise, but because it's owned by a board member, that board member can be punished with an excess benefit transaction.

An excess benefit transaction is defined by the personal benefits that the disqualified person had because of their participation in a nonprofit entity they control. The punishment for a disqualified person can also be an excise tax of 25% of the excess benefit. The disqualified person can also correct their excess benefit transaction plus interest while also replacing material or intellectual property that was gained through the excess benefit transaction. The organization should be left in a financial position not worse than it would be if the law had been followed.

If the property being returned isn't in good condition, the disqualified person will have to make an additional cash payment amounting to that difference. Likewise, the organization must pay the disqualified person the difference if the value of the property exceeds the correction amount.

There are also penalties for other organizational managers who took part in the excess benefit transaction if it's proved that they know what was going on. This includes an excess tax of 10% over the excess benefit, amounting to a maximum of $20,000. That penalty is not applicable if the parties can prove they didn't know they were breaking the law.

Excess benefit transactions don't always happen in bad faith. Many times, the people involved don't even know they're infringing the law. Maybe the owner of the sports equipment store didn't have profit in mind and only suggested his business because it was reliable. That doesn't mean that what he did was right. When he found out that the board was going to vote on where to buy sports equipment, his duty was to excuse himself from that decision, thus avoiding conflicts of interest. If the board voted and chose his store, his absence from the meeting would make the deal more reputable.

# Chapter 6:
# Is Your Nonprofit Achieving Its Goals?

Your work should be based on meeting people's needs that were so far unmet. Designing, implementing, and evaluating programs is a way of achieving that. A program is the sum of coordinated activities that allow you to provide a service. They are aligned with the organization's mission and have to be coordinated with maximum efficiency to avoid wasting time and resources.

Programs may seem chaotic when seen for a distance. For example, while planning the program, you might identify other goals that need to be reached. If reasonable, they should be included in your schedule. In the case your goal has been reached, but you feel the program could continue benefiting people, discuss that possibility.

Don't confuse programs with activities. They are much more tightly organized and focused. An example of an activity would be getting a box full of books and donating all of them to a library. A program would be putting together a system to collect donated books, which would be separated according to themes and reading ages, then using those selections to send them to the libraries where they fit the best.

## The Parts of A Program

A nonprofit program is divided into four parts: inputs, processes, outputs, and outcomes. They are intertwined with each other and can't exist independently. To understand how these phases work, we are going to use the previous example regarding donations of books to libraries:

Program inputs include the resources you need to run the program. For example, in the library's case, you would need paid staff to contact book donors, physical space to store those books, transportation to take them to each library, etc.

The process is the way you deliver the service. For example, books being collected and separated and libraries expanding their collection.

Outputs are the unit of service. Here, it's the books being donated.

Outcomes describe the impact that your work is providing to the people receiving it. Outcomes should be divided into:

- Short-term outcomes: encouraging people to read more by offering them free books.

- Intermediate outcomes: improving school grading, helping people to find new interests as they read more and more, improving reader's grammar and vocabulary, stimulating free thought, etc.

- Long-term outcomes: readers can choose new careers based on what they read, encouraging their own children to read.

While all these parts are equally important, they should all work towards the outcome, which is their meaning to exist. So whenever you're trying to sell a program, use the outcome as your major selling point. Not only does it provide a more cohesive snapshot of your plan, but it also has an idealistic flair to it that will make people want to invest in you.

Each program you implement should aim to achieve a strategic goal, and it should contribute to your organization's mission. Sometimes that means having to drop an entire program because it isn't a fit for you. But, on the other hand, the mission itself can be turned into a major program that will spawn other smaller ones, all working towards the same idea.

You can start the planning of your nonprofit program by creating a simple logic model, in which you include the tops above. Be realistic while listing your outcomes because you'll have to live up to them. Use numbers and statistics in that section, for example, how many books will be donated to how many libraries.

## Strategic Planning

Nonprofits need a strategic plan as a map to achieve their objectives. Each element of your plan should connect to each other. That process can feel chaotic, and it helps if you have an idea of where you're going.

The program description should have a detailed description of the type of business you're conducting, the type of service being provided, the target market, and an overview of your promotion strategies. Include financial details as well of how much you plan to charge and spend. Even though your goal isn't to profit from the program, you shouldn't have financial losses either.

If you are the kind of person who likes to do everything by yourself, get ready to change your life. You can't create a strategy and implement a strategic plan without collaborators.

You should involve the staff in the program planning since they will be the ones that will be implementing it. Those who work at the street level of a nonprofit organization often know more about the people being benefited, for they are dealing with them face to face. If a staff member comes to you with an idea for a new program, you should hear what they have to say.

The board should also be involved in the program planning since this is a responsibility that involves the company's mission. The programs can't happen without their authorization and can't be carried on without their guidance. If it's necessary for them to vote on implementing a program, having an uneven number of board members prevents a tied vote.

Your program plans should also involve the people you are planning to benefit from. They should be allowed to present their own data, expose their needs, and offer you ideas on how to implement that program. For example, if the libraries in our sample are not interested in romantic novels, it's better not to accept them with donations. Or else we would end up with a box of books we have no use for.

Programs work as a living organism that involves everyone in the organization. They should be more than the sum of its parts. For example, you could collect the book donations but wouldn't have a place where people could read them. The library has the physical space, but it needs more books. Together, you both can achieve what you couldn't by yourselves.

You can develop a program in coordination with another one you're already implementing. The first one can be a way of testing waters, so you can start investing in more elaborate ideas. For example, since we are creating a program to encourage young people to read, why not create a literary award to encourage them to write as well? Why not work together with a local school to make that happen?

Listen to everyone you're working with. Fresh and interesting ideas can come from places you never imagined. After finishing a draft of your program, summon a meeting with all your employees to discuss it. You can invite representatives of your client's organizations to examine your plans and provide feedback.

Try not to be a perfectionist. Issues will arise as you implement the program. Don't despair: there's no such thing as a perfect plan. The ideal program is one where everyone can work to the best of their capabilities and provide a positive result. It needs to be aligned with your mission and strategies, and it must offer solutions to your client's problems. Be ready to improvise if things don't go according to plan, and everything should fall into place.

Always try to be innovative and incorporate new concepts for your program, just as for-profits do with their projects. Since your mission is to improve people's lives, you should always improve your methods as well.

Social media is an important tool for you to market your work. A platform you never heard of can be your main vehicle in a week. You can use it to find the clients you are going to serve and learn about their needs. Many nonprofits were born from interactions in social media, when people who cared about a cause learned about each other and cooperated—sometimes without ever meeting each other.

Each target market is going to have its own needs, so it's important that you understand who you will be helping before you start a program. This will help you to evaluate your services and know where to direct your efforts, be it advertising, PR, or selling a service.

You can also use social media to learn about your competitors, find out how their programs compete with yours, their strengths and weaknesses, their prices, etc. Again, this is a case where you can use the transparency required for nonprofits to your advantage. Charity organizations aren't competitive by nature, unlike other fields, but there could be some conflict if two or more organizations are working in the same field at the same time.

## Your Program's Identity

Picking the name of your service can be as hard as picking the name of your organization. If you plan to offer that service for a long time, it's important to create something strong and catchy.

The name shouldn't be associated with a different product or service, from other companies, or from your own. It needs to serve the service you plan to offer now, but if your organization grows large and reaches other places, you should still be able to use it. It's best to avoid names related to geographical places, for example, naming it after a city.

Brainstorming the name of the program with people working on it should offer interesting ideas. For example, some companies conduct polls online, asking people to vote on a list of names. You can also work with focus groups, registering their reactions to names on a list, and asking them to write their impressions about it.

Registering your project's name under a trademark will prevent other organizations from using its name. A name and logo that are used regularly are already protected by common law trademark, at least in the region you use them.

You can get extra protection by registering your nonprofit trademark. This will guarantee protection in all fifty states, which is extra helpful if you're looking to expand nationally. You will have indisputable proof of ownership, rights, and access to federal courts. In addition, if someone infringes on your mark, you are entitled to damages, as legal costs will be paid with the profits the accuser got from using your property.

Trademarks aren't cheap to maintain, and you should do proper research before deciding to do it. Consulting with a specialist is always a good idea. Depending on your budget, consider sticking with the common law trademark mentioned above.

## Delivering Services

With your goal defined and solid marketing planned, the demand for your services should grow. That means you need to increase productivity and check the resources that you need to continue providing that service. Then, make a projection if the demand will continue to increase in the following weeks, months, and years, and ask yourself how long you can maintain that productivity.

You should try to foresee this growth in your marketing analysis, but these things can be impossible to predict. External factors can make the demand for a product or service explode in one minute and fade away in one second.

The distribution services of your nonprofit should always work at the best of their capacity. This is important in any situation, and it could mean life or death when you are producing a critical service, like food or medical aid.

Some services can be provided by phone or online, which is helpful if you are aiding a region that's hard to access. However, if you are constantly moving things around and need to go long distances, it could be a good idea to purchase a vehicle for your organization.

There are charitable car dealers that may offer a donation as a vehicle. Others may not offer you a car free of charge but will give your nonprofit a substantial discount. Donations can also come in the form of old cars, trucks, and vans offered by members of the community. Most of the time, they aren't in the best shape but can be restored.

Some companies choose to conduct a pilot program before committing to an official one. This pilot would be a six-month to one-year program, where you can experiment and see how your ideas will work in practice. Every aspect of the pilot program should be monitored to collect information and data that will be used in full-blown programs.

## Evaluating the Success Of A Program

Part of the program-building is to define what will be the indicators of your success. If your program has deviated from its original idea doesn't always mean it was a failure. It could mean that it evolved and developed into something that better fit the needs of the community.

Programs should be evaluated once a year. This serves not only to rate their efficiency to reach its goals and outcomes but also to plan how they can be improved. Evaluations also guarantee the nonprofit's public trust to let donors know that their contribution is being properly used.

Many decisions depend on these evaluations. Be sure to monitor the programs individually and the revenue and expenses of each one. The overall numbers of the organization might say one thing, but the individual data of these projects can give you a different understanding of your finances.

Having your key indicators planned will allow you to monitor their progress. Have they cost more or less than what you planned? Could you improve this program by hiring or firing someone? Are there any indicators that this program is going to present a financial problem in the long term? How is this program impacting the image of your organization to the public? If a program isn't delivering somehow, the board will have to decide on whether to fix it or cancel it. If it's going well, increase the investment in it.

While it would be ideal that every nonprofit would conduct thorough evaluations of its programs once a year, some of them are too small and don't have the resources and qualified personnel to do it. That job needs to be done somehow, even if you can't hire an accountant to do it. There are some tricks you can employ to prepare your evaluation.

A good strategy is to picture the ideal scenario in which the program would be fully functional and accomplish all its goals. Next, list the aspects of that perfect scenario: the number of employees, the cash flow, the social media following, etc. Then work backward, trying to find out what needs to be improved to achieve those aspects.

Always listen to your staff when conducting an evaluation. They are the best indicators of the issues that a program could have and of how it could be fixed. Numbers and spreadsheets can be misleading, while the people who are in the front doing the hard work can give you precious and authentic insight.

All that information should be presented to a program review team, which should include the chief executive and the involved program directors. You should also include at least one of the people responsible for the original program plan, so they can assess the changes made during the program's implementation.

# Chapter 7:
# Protecting and Growing Your Nonprofit

Protecting your nonprofit is a principle that can assume many forms. It goes from putting a warning sign on a wet floor to securing your financial stability. Managing risks for your nonprofit means spotting and preventing future events that could threaten your organization. If you manage risks correctly, you can create strategies to alleviate these future events and help to keep your nonprofit on track.

According to the Alliance for Nonprofit Management, risk management can be defined as "...a discipline for dealing with the possibility that some future event will cause harm. It provides strategies, techniques, and an approach to recognizing and confronting any threat faced by an organization in fulfilling its mission" (Layne, 2021).

Examples of risk management include:

- Fixing a water or gas leak that could cause accidents in the future.

- Conducting a strict check on a job candidate's background to make sure they are as qualified as they claim to be.

- Creating backups of important data that can be accessible in case the computer system breaks down.

- Setting aside a money reserve that can be used if a company's revenue stream is interrupted.

- Conducting regular maintenance service on the company's vehicle to avoid accidents.

In order to conduct a risk assessment, you need to create an inventory with all the data collected by your nonprofit. By analyzing that data, you can spot potential future risks. Some risks will be more challenging to prevent than others, but their impact on your organization would be worse if you fell victim to them.

Some risks must be taken, and the most you can do is try to soften them. You should know how comfortable you would be with each risk you have to take. Then, establish an oversight and define the steps that you need to take in the time you have until then. That could mean improving your budget in a certain area, offering training to your staff, or purchasing insurance.

Emergencies are prone to happen at any moment, and you need to be prepared for them. The concept of emergency is an unexpected situation with dangerous consequences that require immediate action. There are three key aspects of emergency control in a nonprofit:

- Eliminate risks to prevent emergencies from happening

- Devising procedures to be employed in case an emergency happens

- Conduct training drills with your entire staff to prepare them in advance

Drills are often seen as a waste of time, especially when they happen on a busy day. Still, they are the best way of testing, in a secure environment, how people would react amid an emergency. Not only are the security procedurals tested but also the structure of the building and how to navigate through it in an extreme situation.

Some nonprofits have an emergency plan team among their staff that act as leaders to the rest of the team. Their work goes from elaborating evacuation routes to take care of the federal security forms.

This shouldn't interfere with their daily work, but it helps to make the safety measures work.

## Getting Insurance Coverage

Finding an insurance agent or broker you can trust is a challenge. A good idea is to look for an insurance company that understands the differences between nonprofits and other kinds of business. In addition, it's better to find an agency that specializes in your type of business rather than going for the most well-advertised ones.

Your insurance needs may vary but having general liability insurance is a good start. The special needs of your organization, such as the building you operate, will lead you to purchase specialized kinds of insurance. Whenever you're conducting an event in another organization's building, make sure that they have insurance and that it covers you and your team.

There are two kinds of insurance you could buy: liability insurance and property insurance. Liability insurance will protect your organization from claims regarding negligent conduct. This kind of insurance is divided into:

- Commercial general liability: regarding personal injury, bodily injury, property damage, and advertising injury.

- Business auto: regarding any injuries caused by the company's vehicles. They protect the driver and the owner of the vehicle.

- Directors' and officers' liability: protects the embers of the company from wrongful acts caused by their work in the organization.

- Workers' compensation: covering any liability associated with paid employees.

- Umbrella or excess liability policy: provides limits on liability to avoid excessive loss.

Property insurance includes:

- Crime or employee dishonesty: covers theft made by employees and could also be extended to volunteer workers. It can also include fidelity bonds that will protect you from embezzlement.

- Business owner's package policy: combines the general liability, property, and crime coverages into a single policy.

## What Could Go Wrong?

As a nonprofit runner, you will have to account for every cent you pay. Your responsibility is to use the donors' contributions for the causes they contributed for. It's a constant pressure, and there are several things that could go wrong.

Any business that deals with money and goods is subjected to theft. You could be ripped off at any moment by your employees, board members, or even your clients. Someone could snatch a book from a shelf or embezzle most of your budget for the month. That's one reason you need to account for everything that's happening inside your organization. Be careful even with the people you trust the most.

Regulatory compliance can also be an issue if you have to pay a fine to the IRS. They keep a close look at every move made by nonprofits, and any misstep could mean losing your tax-exempt status. So keeping your forms up to date is also a way of risk management, as well as keeping good practices such as the ones we've seen in the previous chapters.

Another risk you need to keep an eye on is fundraising fraud: people who use your company's name to raise money for a fake cause. Unfortunately, most people don't go through the trouble of fact-checking the material they get in their emails and social media and will donate to these scammers who will keep the money and disappear. This is bad for the donors but also for your company, which will have its name dragged through the mud.

The data you store in your organization's system must be confidential. Your donors and collaborators offer their data trusting that you have a system to keep it secure. That includes financial data for e-commerce, personal records, and information, lists of newsletter subscribers and patrons, etc.

If someone invades your computers, that confidentiality could be jeopardized. Breaching confidential information like that will not only harm the people who own that information but also your organization, which could be held liable. Many nonprofits follow a guide to prevent cybersecurity issues, while others don't even know what that means. Most organizations don't take cybersecurity seriously until they are victims of a crime.

While starting a new business, it's common to buy secondhand equipment such as computers because of their lower price. However, make sure you have those computers formatted, especially if you don't know the previous owner, so you won't end up with compromising material in your office.

The only thing worse than breaching confidential information is to lose a database full of it. This happens not only when someone hacks into your computer and destroys the information but also because your electric system didn't get proper maintenance and made your computer explode or because you dropped water on the keyboard by accident. So what will you do now that all the information you worked so hard to organize is gone?

The only solution is to always keep backup data of all information you store at your nonprofit. Most organizations backup their files in the cloud so they can access them in any part of the world. Together with cloud storage, it's also advisable to keep a hard copy in a USB or external driver. Remember that technology is always changing. People used to store data in huge floppy disks, which are useless nowadays. Tomorrow a new device could show up that would render useless the methods we have now.

Risk management will help you understand future threats but also future opportunities. It will allow you to plan and understand the problems before they arise. It's a powerful tool that will help your organization to move forward, and it gives you an idea of your future performance.

To get that idea of the future, you will need to understand where your company stands in the present. That includes the current and past work you've done, as well as your strengths and weaknesses. With that in mind, you can establish a timeline of where you want to go.

Creating that plan will take time and effort, so don't think you'll be able to have it figured out in one meeting. Every decision you make should be based on facts and data, and you shouldn't try to guess the future, no matter how close it is and how promising or dreadful it looks.

## Doing Right by Others

Reputation means the way your company is seen by public perception. You can spend years building a nonprofit from the ground up, be up to date with the IRS, and offer your community a vital service—but all of that can be destroyed if your reputation is dragged through the mud.

Scandals can come in many forms, from sexual harassment to embezzlement. You might not even be aware of them, but if they happen within your staff or in your office, it could change everything. Donors, old and new, won't support a nonprofit that has a bad reputation. Volunteers will abandon ship, and so will the staff and board members. So what can you do in this situation?

The first thing is to showcase your commitment to the cause and show honesty and accountability. Don't interrupt your work, or people will start associating your organization's name purely with the scandal. Instead, try to get some good press by creating new and improved projects and mentioning how many people are being benefited.

Find out what people are talking about you on the street and on the internet. Social media is often used to destroy reputations. Some people will believe in anything that pops up on the screen of their phones and will spread lies faster than you can deny them.

It's not always lies, though. Whether you're having a scandal or a complaint about a subpar service, you need to be honest about your actual responsibility. In a situation like that, it's better to find a solution with the persons involved. On the other hand, if the problem is angry comments with foul language on the internet, it's better to ignore the whole matter.

Negative feedback can be valid and help you grow as a company. If someone has something meaningful to say, listen to it. And if their lawyer is going to be present, bring yours as well. Not everything has to go to court, and it's possible to reach a deal before the situation becomes irreversible.

Speaking to the press about accusations made by third parties is a delicate thing. No one in the organization should talk in public about an issue before conducting a proper internal investigation. A well-written press release should be your main channel of communication with the media, representing not one person but the organization.

If the cameras are impossible to avoid, select a handful of people to represent you. That person should have an important role in the organization, such as a board member or an influential member of the staff. It's necessary to pass a solid and serious image, speak with good diction, and be prepared to answer questions without trying to fool anyone or telling lies.

Do your best to give a positive image, and avoid using anyone as a scapegoat, even if they're guilty. People will see this as a lack of loyalty between the organization and the employee. When asked trick questions, say that you are going to answer them in a press release you'll send to the press.

## Growing Your Nonprofit

A nonprofit organization can start with a couple of people with a dream and become something much larger with time. However, nonprofits are living organisms, and they need to be fed in order to grow. Money and qualified personnel are important, but they alone won't make your organization grow as much as it could.

Find out about a similar nonprofit that's ahead of yours and try to learn how they grew. Don't copy their strategies; they won't work the same for you. Instead, use them as an inspiration to create your own models and strategies that are tailored to fit your organization.

Since your resources are limited and could vary drastically from one month to the next, learning to do more with less is important. Find a balance between efficiency and resourcefulness, and don't spread yourself and your staff too thin.

There are simple ideas that cost nothing, for example, having your employees adding the company's logo to their social media photos. It costs nothing, spreads the name of the organization, and creates a good image of people who are proud of the place where they work or volunteer.

Getting involved in the community isn't just about serving the needs of a demographic. Your perfect volunteer could be right next to you, but you won't see them if you're shut in your office reading resumes. So instead, go to the places where people gather, such as churches, carnivals, volunteer fairs, and mission fairs, and you could find out about men and women who could make a difference to your cause.

With so many nonprofits asking for people's money, most people will prefer to donate to an organization they already have a link to, such as a friend and a relative. Use that influence. Your board and staff should all contact their families and friends, and every time you hire someone new, instruct them to do the same. The donations might not be substantial, but you will add a good number of names to your list of donors.

Getting money from business can be harder than from individuals. As a result, they will be more inclined to offer donations as services and offer free advertising space. They can also offer space on their buildings to collect donations from their customers. That can be more effective in a place where people come and go all day than it would be at the nonprofit's building.

You will hear plenty of negative responses from donors, but that doesn't mean that you shouldn't call them again in the future. There are people who think that all nonprofits are scams and that you will be using the money for your own benefit. But there might also be people who cannot offer you a donation today but will in a few months. Always be gentle with these donors, ask them when you can call again, and keep their names and the date in your organizer.

New opportunities appear at every moment, and you must be ready to talk about your nonprofit. You might be in an airport queue or in the dentist's waiting room when someone asks what you do for a living. This is a golden chance, and you should talk with enthusiasm about what you do, how you do it, how much it impacts people's lives, and how much you believe in your work.

If the stranger is interested and wants to tell his own story, don't interrupt him. Instead, connect his story to yours. At the end of the talk, offer your business card. This should be common practice among all people in the organization. Try to make it natural, not rehearsed, or else you'll lose interest.

Great for building awareness of your work is to put together presentations in public events. You might not fill an auditorium by yourself, but getting permission to talk for a few minutes before a play or a concert will make your nonprofit known to many diverse people.

People don't donate to a cause they just heard of; they donate to a cause that they've heard about several times. Be patient and persistent, and you'll see they will act. Your donors aren't just people who write checks; they're an integral part of the organization. It's the inspiration to help that brought them, and you need to feed that inspiration if you want them to keep coming back.

The way you tell your story can convince people to offer you monthly donations. Instead of asking for a large donation to conduct a big project, you can convince them that small regular payments will help to do the job in the long run.

## Valuing Your Staff

Volunteers deserve respect and professionalism. These people will be giving you their time and workforce because they believe in what you do. They work for free because serving the mission is their salary. When you have an open position for a paid job, you can hire someone whose abilities you already tested as a volunteer.

Every volunteer should receive a handbook at the start of their work. The first thing to be included in this handbook is a heartfelt thank you from the people in charge of the organization. They should be informed about the volunteer philosophy, which will make them feel how important their work is, and the work conditions they will operate in. Make the volunteers feel at home, and they will give you their best efforts in return.

Talent can also be found at the top of the pyramid. Think of what your board members can bring to the table. Maybe they have skills that can help the organization to grow. Perhaps they have a contact that will make a difference in the work you're doing. Don't think of your board members as passive players who are only there to vote and offer their image to the organization; in a nonprofit, every part is a moving part!

# Chapter 8:
# Templates and Forms

## *Form 1023 – Application for Recognition of Exemption under Section 501.c3*

Access www.irs.gov/.

Click on Forms and Instructions.

Make a search for 1023.

Follow the instructions to fill in the form.

Follow the same instructions to access Form 2013-EZ, which can be filed online.

## *Form 990 – Return of Organization Exempt from Income Tax*

Access www.irs.gov/.

Click on Forms and Instructions.

Type 990 in the search bar.

Select the form that fits your needs, keeping in mind that the EZ version can be filed online.

You can find Form 990-T for Exempt Organization Business Income Tax Return through the same method.

# *Articles of Incorporation Template*

Articles of incorporation are used for corporations to get legal recognition as a business entity. Below is a template for such a document, which can be found on the website LegalTemplates.net (2020):

Achilles of Incorporation of _____

(Under the Business Corporation Law of _____ [State])

FIRST: The name of the corporation is _____ [Full legal corporation name].

SECOND: The principal place of business of the corporation is _____ [Address].

THIRD: The name and address of the registered agent is _____[Agent],_____ _____ [Address].

FOURTH: The purpose for which the corporation is organized is

_____

FIFTH: The corporation is authorized to issue a total number of _____ shares of (Check one)

☐ Common ☐ Preferred ☐ Other: _____ stock: (Check one)

☐ Without par value.

☐ With a par value of $_____ per share.

SIXTH: The name and address of the director(s) is:

Name:_____ Address: _____

Name:_____ Address: _____

Name:_____ Address: _____

Name:_____ Address: _____

Name:_____ Address: _____

The name and address of the officer(s) is:

Name:_____ Address: _____

Name:_____ Address: _____

Name:_____ Address: _____

Name:_____ Address: _____

Name:_____ Address: _____

SEVENTH: The name and address of the incorporator is _____[Incorporator],_____ [Address].

EIGHTH: The period of duration of the Corporation: (Check one)

☐ Is perpetual.

☐ Is _____ years.

☐ Ends on _____ [Date].

IN WITNESS WHEREOF, the undersigned has executed these Articles of Incorporation on this _____ day of _____, 20_____.


Signature of Incorporator


Date


Print Name of Incorporator


Capacity/Title: Incorporator

133

## *Conflict of Interest Policy Template*

You will need a written code that details what constitutes a conflict of interest inside your organization. The website BoardSource (2015) offers a full-length version of the contract, which includes the disclosure questionnaire bellow:

CONFLICT-OF-INTEREST DISCLOSURE STATEMENT

A. I have no knowledge of any interest, relationship, or situation regarding me or my XYZ organization that might result in a conflict of interest between us.

B. Below are lists of relationships and interests involving me as a member of this organization that I believe could result in actual, apparent, or potential conflicts of interest between me and the other members of XYZ:

Corporate (nonprofit and for-profit) directorships, positions, and employment:

_____

Organizations in which I have membership:

_____

Organizations where I have contracts, business activities, and investments:

_____

Other relationships and activities:

_____

My primary business or occupation at the time of signing:

_____

Having read and understood the Conflict-of-Interest Policy of XYZ, I agree to be bound by it. The board chair of XYZ will be promptly informed of any relevant change in the information here contained.

| _____ | _____ | _____ |
| Type/Print Name | Signature | Date |

## *Gift Acceptance Policy Template*

The Council of Nonprofits presents several versions of the gift acceptance policy, which can be a simple document. Here's an example:

Gift Acceptance Policy

1. [Organization Name] solicits and accepts gifts that are consistent with its mission.

2. Donations will generally be accepted from individuals, partnerships, corporations, foundations, government agencies, or other entities without limitations.

3. In the course of its regular fundraising activities, [Organization Name] will accept donations of money, real property, personal property, stock, and in-kind services.

4. Certain types of gifts must be reviewed prior to acceptance due to the special liabilities they may pose for [Organization Name]. Examples of gifts that

will be subject to review include gifts of real property, gifts of personal property, and gifts of securities.

## *Fundraising Letter Instructions*

In order to ask for funds from donors or grants, you need to be convincing about the problem at hand and how your organization is the best to handle it. Therefore, make sure that your letter includes the following steps:

Define the problem and the solution you want to implement. Having a catchy name for the project is valuable here.

Reveal your goals to show the reader that you know exactly where and how you are going to use their donation.

Tell the reader about the previous work that your nonprofit has done in that field and how that experience will count in the project at hand.

Present a narrative of the community's problem and talk about the people whose lives you will be impacting.

Ask for money. You should be blunt about how much you need and what you are going to do with this. Make the reader feel that their donation is valuable.

## *Business Plan Template*

This business plan template is based on a model created by Lena Eisenstein (2020) and can be found in full detail on the Board Effect website.

Name of Nonprofit:

Primary Contact:

Physical Address:

Mailing Address:

Telephone Number:

Website URL:

Email Address:

Table of Contents (include page numbers)

Executive Summary

Include information about your organization's mission and history in a tone that engages the reader and motivates them to continue reading.

Products, Programs, and Services

Highlight the products and services you offer and plan to offer in the future. Illustrate the impact of your work and how the donations help it.

Marketing Plan

Offer a description of your marketing research, constituency, competitors and collaborators, and strategy. Include research and identify your demographic and identify your competitors and collaborators. Then, explain your promotions, advertising, budgeting, and marketing methods.

Operational Plan

Give an idea of the day-to-day work in your nonprofit. List your permits, licenses, insurance coverage, trademarks, patents, and copyrights. Add a description of your staff's roles and responsibilities. Include the number of employees, type of employees, pay structure, and whether you use contractors or freelancers. Explain whether you will need to hire new staff and when you're projected to start hiring.

Impact Plan

Describe your nonprofit's plan to achieve your mission and vision. Inform your donors on how to plan to assess the impact of your efforts.

Financial Plan

Include a summary of your past financial picture and what you hope that your future financial picture will be. Add reports such as cash flow statements, balance sheets, income statements, and your budget. Include a list of your revenue streams, including partners, sponsors, donors, grants, subscriptions, membership fees, and fundraising events. In addition, be sure to list your nonprofit's debts and income, including bonds, holdings, and endowments.

## *Nonprofit Press Release Instructions*

You should make your press release short, and it's better to keep it to a single page. Start with the date at the top of the page.

Add a short title that describes what you want to promote. Keep it simple and strong.

Below that, add a brief compliment, which works a lot better if you know the name of the specific reporter you're sending it to.

In three paragraphs, summon up the event, telling what is happening, when it's happening, and why they should make a story about it.

Finish with a thank you and your name.

## *Volunteer Application Form Template*

Volunteers are a blessing, but you want to know as much as you can about them before letting them into your organization. Knowing some details about people before hiring them makes this decision easier. This template, together with many others, can be found at Template.net:

Volunteer Application Form

Contact Information

Name:

Street Address:

City, ST ZIP Code:

Home Phone:

Work Phone:

Email Address:

Availability

When are you available for volunteer assignments?

___ :_____ to ___:_____ Monday

___ :_____ to ___:_____ Tuesday

___ :_____ to ___:_____ Wednesday

___ :_____ to ___:_____ Thursday

___ : _____ to ___ : _____ Friday

___ : _____ to ___ : _____ Saturday

Interests

In which areas are you best suited to volunteer?

___ AIDS/HIV ___ Homelessness/Hunger ___ Environment

___ Children and Youth ___ Volunteer Leadership ___ Health/ Wellness

___ Disaster Assistance ___ Building/ Repair ___ Seniors

___ Fundraising ___ Disability Services ___ Youth Volunteering

## Special Skills or Qualifications

Skills and qualifications can be acquired through employment, previous volunteer work, or other activities such as hobbies or sports. What skills or qualifications do you have as a volunteer?

Previous Volunteer Experience

Have you worked as a volunteer before? If so, what did you do?

Person to Notify in Case of Emergency

Name:

Street Address:

City, ST ZIP Code:

Home Phone:

Work Phone:

Email Address:

Our Policy:

This organization follows a policy that offers equal opportunities regardless of race, color, gender, age, sexual preference, religion, national origin, or disability.

We appreciate the time you took to fill this form and wish you good luck.

---

## *Volunteer Handbook Instructions*

According to Tobi Johnson (2013), a volunteer handbook should contain the following elements:

A letter of gratitude from the organization's leader.

Info about your organization, including your mission and past services.

Philosophy of the volunteer program, where volunteers get to know about the importance of their work.

Ethics guidelines, including inside work ethic and the basics of nonprofit laws.

Working conditions, including safety and accessibility.

Customer service standards, informing on how to serve the public.

Required paperwork and reporting, with special attention to confidentiality.

Training procedures, schedule, and expectations.

Perks offered to volunteers.

Supervision and support, requirements of attendance, reasons for dismissal.

Volunteer feedback.

Volunteer protections and insurance coverage.

Resources and materials.

Attachments.

## *Letter of Inquiry Instructions*

Your letter of inquiry should include:

An introduction, including the name of your organization, your budget, and a description of the project.

The organization description, which should inform why you are the best choice to do that job. Describe your past and current programs.

The statement of need is where you must convince the reader that there's an urgent need and that your project can meet it. Use storytelling strategies to create a narrative where you can fit technical information.

The methodology must fit the information you gave so far, showing how you plan to proceed to solve that issue.

Add a list of other funding sources that you plan to approach for this project.

A final summary where you make yourself available to answer any questions and thank the reader for their time.

## *Corporate Letter Request for Gift in Kind*

Subject: Your help is needed to raise funds for [nonprofit mission]!

Dear [donor's name],

I am [name, position] of [name of the organization]. We at [name of the organization] are seeking help to [organization mission] by [actions you have done so far. This is a good place to add a touching story about an individual you helped, adding that many others need similar help.]

While we are proud of our many achievements, [name of the organization] still has a long path ahead of it.

Right now, we're gathering support for [the name of the new project that you are fundraising].

We would like to count on your kind help in the form of [donation amount, be it in money, items, or services]. This will help us to further the cause and impact the lives of many people.

We would be happy to answer any questions you have and give you more information about the work we do at [name of the organization]. Our doors are always open to you, in case you want to visit our office for a cup of coffee.

Your donation makes a huge difference to the people we support. With your help, we can [insert the ways you plan to use the donations and the impact of the donation of this specific contributor]. If you choose to contribute, just fill the attached form or call us at [phone number].

Every donation means the world to us! Together, we are closer to reach [insert goal]!

Sincerely,

[name]

[nonprofit website]

[email]

## *Grant Proposal Instructions*

A successful grant proposal should include the following elements:

Cover letter, in which you briefly present your organization's mission and history.

Evaluation, in which you inform how you are going to evaluate and make sure that the investments are going to be well spent.

Needs assessment, in which you inform how you plan to make your organization achieve its ideal state.

Executive summary, in which you go into detail about your history and mission. The information should go deeper than the cover letter.

Methods and strategies: the most essential part of the proposal, where you present an over.

Sustainability plan, in which you will show that the required grant is going to fulfill the needs of the program you desire to implement, and a view of how you plan to use the grant to fulfill each need of the organization.

Budget, in which you present a spreadsheet in accordance with the information that you provided in the sustainability plan.

## *Annual Report*

Access www.irs.gov/.

Click Charities & Nonprofits.

Click Finding Filings Forms

Click 990-series forms and schedules.

Select the type of form that fits your needs.

# Conclusion

Doing something with love isn't always a guarantee that we're doing it right. For example, every day we see businesses closing in our neighborhoods. That's because their owners knew how to do their work well—bake bread, fix computers, offer dentistry services—but didn't take the time to educate themselves about the business side of things.

If you love something, you need to continue insisting on it even after the initial enthusiasm is gone. Many people start their journey to create a nonprofit with a bright dream in their hearts. Unfortunately, that dream soon becomes a nightmare, for they weren't ready to face the difficulties that this kind of work involves.

When someone thinks of creating a nonprofit to improve children's education, they think of the children smiling with books in their hands. The company's mission seems bigger than everything until you get a mountain of forms, laws, bylaws, regulations, audits, annual reports, and everything that seems to trap you in a bureaucracy.

The obstacles in the path of creating and running a nonprofit organization are many. There are several things that could go wrong, be it by negligence or inexperience, and that can impact your life permanently. In addition, not everyone is ready for the responsibility of running such an organization.

Knowing all of that shouldn't discourage you. Being aware of how things could go wrong is a giant step towards being able to do it right. If before reading this book you didn't know what a Form 990 was, how to conduct a risk assessment, and the difference between a program and an activity, now you're a little more prepared to work on your dream of running a nonprofit.

Common advice among people of many businesses is to find a mentor that will guide you through your professional journey. Mentors aren't easy to find, though. Even if you know someone who has experience in the field and will share it with you, it's not always possible to find the time and resources to learn all they offer.

We wish, with this book, to provide mentorship to those whose desire to do good wasn't backed by experience in the field. We are aware that some people would be scared by the processes and consequences of infringing on them. However, it wouldn't be fair to pretend that the world of nonprofits didn't include these things.

Still, the reality is that it is possible to open and run a nonprofit, getting and maintaining your 501(c)(3) status, selecting a board, hiring and training staff and volunteers, and conducting your daily work as a way of serving a mission for the good of your community. It is possible, and if you keep both your feet on the ground and prepare yourself for the difficulties, you can—and should—do it!

Tax exemption is a key reason why nonprofits can continue to operate. The regulations that oversee these organizations are what prevent this system from being abused. Try to look at the IRS as a partner, not an enemy. Keeping them up-to-date with your operations is what they ask in exchange for offering you this advantage.

If by reading this book you decided not to enter this world as a founder, there's no shame in that. You can still help people by donating, volunteering, and even working as a staff or board member in an existing nonprofit. You can use the resources that you learned here to figure out which organization better fits your ideals. Who knows if, with time, that desire to start an organization of your own won't surface again?

For the people who have finished this book and are adamant about their decision to create and running a non-profit, we are proud of you. The journey is just beginning, and you will learn a lot of things that don't fit in a book. The path is rocky, and from time to time, you will think of giving up. When that happens, come back to these pages and remember how that path started.

How long that journey might take, always be proud of what you are doing. All our lives, we are being told that people are no good and that nobody does anything unless they can take some advantage out of it.

Here you are, getting educated on how to start an enterprise that will take blood, sweat, and tears and offer you little money in exchange. You are moved by the desire to make the world a better place, and now you have the tools and the knowledge to start that journey.

Whatever you're doing in the future, posing for photos for magazines or filing tax-exemption documents in your office in the middle of the night, wear that pride like a gold medal, and don't let anyone take it away from you.

Now go and give it your best!

# References

5 Tips for Hiring Nonprofit Staff. Www.travelers.com,
www.travelers.com/resources/business-
industries/nonprofit/5-tips-for-hiring-nonprofit-staff.
Accessed 19 July 2021.

10+ Volunteer Application Template - Word, PDF | Free &
Premium Templates. Www.template.net,
www.template.net/business/application-form-
template/volunteer-application-template/. Accessed 27 July
2021.

26 U.S. Code § 170 - Charitable, Etc., Contributions and
Gifts. LII / Legal Information Institute,
www.law.cornell.edu/uscode/text/26/170#c. Accessed 20
July 2021.

Amanda Foran. How to Grow Your Nonprofit. Nonprofit
Expert, 6 Oct. 2017, www.nonprofitexpert.com/how-to-
grow-your-nonprofit/. Accessed 13 July 2021.

Annual Electronic Filing Requirement for Small Exempt
Organizations — Form 990-N (E-Postcard) | Internal
Revenue Service. Irs.gov, 2014, www.irs.gov/charities-non-
profits/annual-electronic-filing-requirement-for-small-
exempt-organizations-form-990-n-e-postcard. Accessed 27
June 2021.

Articles of Incorporation | Requirements & Free Template.
Legal Templates, 12 Nov. 2020,
legaltemplates.net/form/articles-of-incorporation/. Accessed
27 July 2021.

Auvin, Jodi. Nonprofit Financial Management: Top Ten Things You Need to Know. MissionBox, 2 July 2019, www.missionbox.com/article/107/nonprofit-financial-management-top-ten-things-you-need-to-know. Accessed 13 July 2021.

Avanzato, Joseph. Maintain Separation between a Nonprofit and the Foundation That Supports It. JD Supra, www.jdsupra.com/legalnews/maintain-separation-between-a-nonprofit-15478/. Accessed 15 July 2021.

Averkamp, Harold. Nonprofit Accounting - Statement of Functional Expenses, Statement of Cash Flows | AccountingCoach. AccountingCoach.com, www.accountingcoach.com/nonprofit-accounting/explanation/4#:~:text=The%20statement%20of%20cash%20flows. Accessed 23 July 2021.

Birken, Jess. Nonprofit Myth Busters: Starting a Nonprofit May Not Be Right for You. Birken Law, 26 Jan. 2018, birkenlaw.com/cornerstone-content/nonprofit-myth-busters-starting-nonprofit-may-not-right/. Accessed 13 July 2021.

Blue Insights. The Basics: Intermediate Sanctions and Excess Benefit Transactions. Blue & Co., LLC, 11 Apr. 2018, www.blueandco.com/the-basics-intermediate-sanctions-and-excess-benefit-transactions/. Accessed 26 July 2021.

BoardSource - Empowering Boards & Inspiring Leadership. BoardSource, 28 Dec. 2015, boardsource.org/. Accessed 27 July 2021.

BPlans. Nonprofit. Bplans: Business Planning Resources and Free Business Plan Samples, www.bplans.com/nonprofit-business-plans/. Accessed 13 July 2021.

Carter, Christopher. The Structure of a 501(C)(3) Organization. Small Business - Chron.com, smallbusiness.chron.com/structure-501c3-organization-2763.html. Accessed 13 July 2021.

Charitable Solicitation Registration. National Council of Nonprofits, 12 Jan. 2015, www.councilofnonprofits.org/tools-resources/charitable-solicitation-registration. Accessed 13 July 2021.

Chung, Elizabeth. What Is Peer-To-Peer Fundraising? Classy, 22 Oct. 2014, www.classy.org/blog/what-is-peer-to-peer-fundraising-2/. Accessed 22 July 2021.

Clepper, Rachel. Nonprofit Fundraising Strategies That Will Help You Raise More. Neon One, 30 Oct. 2020, neonone.com/resources/blog/nonprofit-fundraising-strategies/. Accessed 13 July 2021.

Decker, Allie. The Ultimate Guide to Nonprofit Fundraising. Blog.hubspot.com, blog.hubspot.com/marketing/nonprofit-fundraising. Accessed 13 July 2021.

Depreciation | Nonprofit Accounting Basics. Www.nonprofitaccountingbasics.org, 12 June 2009, www.nonprofitaccountingbasics.org/accounting-bookkeeping/depreciation. Accessed 26 July 2021.

Donation Request Letters: What You Need to Say. Fundraising Letters Blog, www.fundraisingletters.org/donation-request-letters/. Accessed 29 July 2021.

Double the Nation. Nonprofit Fundraising: A Complete Overview (20+ Methods!). Double the Donation, 2019, doublethedonation.com/tips/nonprofit-fundraising/. Accessed 13 July 2021.

Eisenstein, Lena. Nonprofit Business Plan Template. BoardEffect, 20 Jan. 2020, www.boardeffect.com/blog/nonprofit-business-plan-template/. Accessed 28 July 2021.

Ellice. 10 Ways to Make Your Website Accessible - DreamHost. Website Guides, Tips and Knowledge, 19 Dec. 2018, www.dreamhost.com/blog/make-your-website-accessible/. Accessed 21 July 2021.

Esq, Audrey Chisholm. Start a 501c3 Nonprofit That Doesn't Ruin Your Life: How to Legally Structure Your Nonprofit to Avoid I.R.S. Trouble, Lawsuits, Financial Scandals & More! Amazon, Greenlight Books & Publishing, LLC, 7 Nov. 2018, www.amazon.com/Start-501c3-Nonprofit-That-Doesnt-ebook/dp/B07KBC4SQZ/. Accessed 13 July 2021.

Everson, Crystal. Should Your Nonprofit Register a Trademark? Www.legalzoom.com, 27 Apr. 2020, www.legalzoom.com/articles/should-your-nonprofit-register-a-trademark#:~:text=If%20your%20nonprofit%20plans%20on. Accessed 28 July 2021.

Expert, Nonprofit. Can Nonprofits Lobby? Nonprofit Expert, 4 June 2012, www.nonprofitexpert.com/nonprofit-questions-answers/can-nonprofits-lobby/. Accessed 21 July 2021.

Federal Filing Requirements for Nonprofits. National Council of Nonprofits, 12 Jan. 2015, www.councilofnonprofits.org/tools-resources/federal-filing-requirements-nonprofits. Accessed 13 July 2021.

Field, Rebecca. Compliance and Documentation: Cornerstones of Effective Grants Management. Www.claconnect.com, 14 Aug. 2017, www.claconnect.com/resources/articles/2017/compliance-and-documentation-cornerstones-of-effective-grants-management. Accessed 26 July 2021.

Foundation Group, Inc. Questions You Must Consider before Starting a Nonprofit. , 13 July 2021.

Free Grant Proposal Template by PandaDoc - Get 2021 Sample. PandaDoc, www.pandadoc.com/grant-proposal-template/. Accessed 29 July 2021.

Fritz, Joanne. How to Create a Gift Range Chart for Your Fundraising Campaign. The Balance MB, 14 Apr. 2020, www.thebalancesmb.com/gift-chart-fundraising-campaigns-2502075. Accessed 13 July 2021.

---. What Is a 501(C)(3) Tax-Exempt Organization? The Balance Small Business, 19 July 2020, www.thebalancesmb.com/what-is-a-501-c-3-tax-exempt-organization-how-do-we-apply-2502154. Accessed 13 July 2021.

---. When Should a Nonprofit Worry about Income Unrelated to Its Mission? The Balance Small Business, 26 Apr. 2020, www.thebalancesmb.com/how-much-unrelated-earned-income-can-a-nonprofit-receive-2501873. Accessed 13 July 2021.

Gardner, Karen. How to Ask Dealerships for Auto Donations for Your Non-Profit Organization. Small Business - Chron.com, 28 Mar. 2019, smallbusiness.chron.com/ask-dealerships-auto-donations-nonprofit-organization-59626.html. Accessed 28 July 2021.

Garry, Joan. Critical Interview Questions for Non Profit Board Members. Joan Garry Nonprofit Leadership, 18 Sept. 2015, blog.joangarry.com/interview-questions-non-profit-board-members/. Accessed 16 July 2021.

Gauss, Allison. 5 Growth Strategies for Small Nonprofits. Classy, 26 June 2015, www.classy.org/blog/5-growth-strategies-for-small-nonprofits/. Accessed 13 July 2021.

getfullyfunded. Core Number Calculator for Fundraising. Get Fully Funded, getfullyfunded.com/core-number-calculator/. Accessed 13 July 2021.

Giacalone, Cary. 7 Best Financial Practices for Nonprofit Organizations. Blog.concannonmiller.com, 13 June 2019, blog.concannonmiller.com/4thought/7-best-financial-practices-for-nonprofit-organizations. Accessed 13 July 2021.

Gift Acceptance Policies. National Council of Nonprofits, 9 Jan. 2015, www.councilofnonprofits.org/tools-resources/gift-acceptance-policies. Accessed 13 July 2021.

Good, Funding For. Donor Relations 101 – What I Learned. Funding for Good, 23 Apr. 2019, fundingforgood.org/donor-relations-101-what-i-learned/. Accessed 13 July 2021.

Harbor Compliance. Fundraising Registration & Compliance | Harbor Compliance. Www.harborcompliance.com, www.harborcompliance.com/information/charitable-registration. Accessed 20 July 2021.

Haskins, Jane. How to Start a Nonprofit. Www.legalzoom.com, 21 Apr. 2021, www.legalzoom.com/articles/how-to-start-a-nonprofit. Accessed 13 July 2021.

Heaslip, Emily. Nonprofit, Not-for Profit & For-Profit Organizations Explained. Https://Www.uschamber.com/Co, 30 Mar. 2020, www.uschamber.com/co/start/strategy/nonprofit-vs-not-for-profit-vs-for-profit. Accessed 13 July 2021.

Holl, Erica. 6 Inspiring Quotes of Advice from Nonprofit Leaders. Charity Charge, 27 Mar. 2018, www.charitycharge.com/inspiring-quotes-from-nonprofit-leaders/. Accessed 27 July 2021.

How to Raise Awareness for Your Nonprofit. Capital Business Solutions, 29 July 2019, www.capitalbusiness.net/resources/how-to-raise-awareness-for-your-nonprofit-organization/. Accessed 13 July 2021.

Huston, Heather. The Benefits of Forming a Nonprofit Company. Www.wolterskluwer.com, 14 Aug. 2020, www.wolterskluwer.com/en/expert-insights/the-benefits-of-forming-a-nonprofit-company. Accessed 15 July 2021.

Hutton, Stan. 10 Tips for Protecting Your Nonprofit. Dummies, www.dummies.com/business/nonprofits/10-tips-for-protecting-your-nonprofit/. Accessed 13 July 2021.

Hutton, Stan, and Frances N. Phillips. Nonprofit Kit for Dummies. Amazon, For Dummies, 12 Dec. 2016, www.amazon.com/Nonprofit-Kit-Dummies-Stan-Hutton-ebook/dp/B01NCMDGK6/. Accessed 13 July 2021.

Ibele, Terry. How to Start a Nonprofit in 4 Parts. Wild Apricot Blog, 20 Aug. 2019, www.wildapricot.com/blog/how-to-start-a-nonprofit#what-are-the-alternatives-to-starting-a-nonprofit-. Accessed 13 July 2021.

---. How to Start a Nonprofit in 4 Parts. Wild Apricot Blog, 20 Aug. 2019, www.wildapricot.com/blog/how-to-start-a-nonprofit#step-2-how-to-build-a-lasting-foundation. Accessed 19 July 2021.

---. How to Start a Nonprofit in 4 Parts. Wild Apricot Blog, 20 Aug. 2019, www.wildapricot.com/blog/how-to-start-a-nonprofit#step-1-three-things-to-research-before-starting-a-nonprofit. Accessed 19 July 2021.

---. How to Start a Nonprofit in 4 Parts. Wild Apricot Blog, 20 Aug. 2019, www.wildapricot.com/blog/how-to-start-a-nonprofit#step-3-what-to-include-in-your-nonprofit-business-plan. Accessed 19 July 2021.

---. How to Start a Nonprofit in 4 Parts. Wild Apricot Blog, 20 Aug. 2019, www.wildapricot.com/blog/how-to-start-a-nonprofit#step-4-your-four-main-sources-of-revenue. Accessed 19 July 2021.

---. How to Start a Nonprofit in 4 Parts. Wild Apricot Blog, 20 Aug. 2019, www.wildapricot.com/blog/how-to-start-a-nonprofit#1-define-success-and-build-job-descriptions. Accessed 19 July 2021.

---. How to Start a Nonprofit in 4 Parts. Wild Apricot Blog, 20 Aug. 2019, www.wildapricot.com/blog/how-to-start-a-nonprofit#1-define-success-and-build-job-descriptions. Accessed 19 July 2021.

---. How to Start a Nonprofit in 4 Parts. Wild Apricot Blog, 20 Aug. 2019, www.wildapricot.com/blog/how-to-start-a-nonprofit#how-much-money-do-you-need-to-start-a-nonprofit-. Accessed 19 July 2021.

---. How to Start a Nonprofit in 4 Parts. Wild Apricot Blog, 20 Aug. 2019, www.wildapricot.com/blog/how-to-start-a-nonprofit#part-.2-setting-up-shop-and-hiring-staff. Accessed 19 July 2021.

---. How to Start a Nonprofit in 4 Parts. Wild Apricot Blog, 20 Aug. 2019, www.wildapricot.com/blog/how-to-start-a-nonprofit#part-3-choosing-nonprofit-software-and-building-your-website. Accessed 19 July 2021.

---. How to Start a Nonprofit in 4 Parts. Wild Apricot Blog, 20 Aug. 2019, www.wildapricot.com/blog/how-to-start-a-nonprofit#which-social-media-channels-you-ll-need-to-set-up-for-your-501c3. Accessed 19 July 2021.

---. How to Start a Nonprofit in 4 Parts. Wild Apricot Blog, 20 Aug. 2019, www.wildapricot.com/blog/how-to-start-a-nonprofit#how-much-money-do-you-need-to-start-a-nonprofit-. Accessed 19 July 2021.

---. How to Start a Nonprofit in 4 Parts. Wild Apricot Blog, 20 Aug. 2019, www.wildapricot.com/blog/how-to-start-a-nonprofit. Accessed 19 July 2021.

---. How to Start a Nonprofit in 4 Parts. Wild Apricot Blog, 20 Aug. 2019, www.wildapricot.com/blog/how-to-start-a-nonprofit. Accessed 19 July 2021.

---. The 5 Best Ways to Generate Earned Income for Your Nonprofit. Wild Apricot Blog, 15 Jan. 2018, www.wildapricot.com/blog/nonprofit-earned-income. Accessed 19 July 2021.

---. The Complete Nonprofit Compliance Checklist from an Expert. Wild Apricot Blog, 28 Sept. 2017, www.wildapricot.com/blog/complete-nonprofit-compliance-checklist#additional-resources. Accessed 19 July 2021.

Ibrisevic, Ilma. Fundraising Letters: Asking for Donations Made Easy (+ Free Template). Nonprofit Blog, 15 June 2021, donorbox.org/nonprofit-blog/fundraising-letters/. Accessed 27 July 2021.

---. How to Hire a Great Nonprofit Executive Director. Nonprofit Blog, 2 Feb. 2018, donorbox.org/nonprofit-blog/hire-great-nonprofit-executive-director/. Accessed 13 July 2021.

Ilma Ibrisevic. How to Start a 501c3 - Ultimate Guide to Registering a 501c3 Nonprofit. Nonprofit Blog, 10 Sept. 2018, donorbox.org/nonprofit-blog/how-to-start-a-501c3/. Accessed 13 July 2021.

Ingram, David. What Are the Benefits of Starting a Non-Profit Organization? Small Business - Chron.com, smallbusiness.chron.com/benefits-starting-non-profit-organization-1663.html. Accessed 13 July 2021.

IRS. About Form 990, Return of Organization Exempt from Income Tax | Internal Revenue Service. Irs.gov, 2019, www.irs.gov/forms-pubs/about-form-990.

---. About Form 1023, Application for Recognition of Exemption under Section 501(C)(3) of the Internal Revenue Code | Internal Revenue Service. Www.irs.gov, www.irs.gov/forms-pubs/about-form-1023.

---. About Form 1023-EZ, Streamlined Application for Recognition of Exemption under Section 501(C)(3) of the Internal Revenue Code | Internal Revenue Service. Www.irs.gov, www.irs.gov/forms-pubs/about-form-1023-ez. Accessed 13 July 2021.

---. Exemption Requirements - 501(C)(3) Organizations | Internal Revenue Service. Irs.gov, 2019, www.irs.gov/charities-non-profits/charitable-organizations/exemption-requirements-501c3-organizations. Accessed 13 July 2021.

Izmailova, Sayana. 5 Things to Consider When Naming Your Nonprofit. Wild Apricot Blog, 30 Oct. 2020, www.wildapricot.com/blog/naming-your-nonprofit#what-s-in-a-name. Accessed 20 July 2021.

Johnson, Tobi. A Volunteer Handbook Sample That Will Help Guide Your Volunteers. 7 Nov. 2013, tobijohnson.com/volunteer-handbook-sample/. Accessed 29 July 2021.

Kagan, Julia. 501(C)(3) Organization Definition. Investopedia, 20 June 2021, www.investopedia.com/terms/1/501c3-organizations.asp. Accessed 13 July 2021.

Kihlstedt, Andrea. Capital Campaign Gift Range Chart: Understanding the Basics. capitalcampaigntoolkit.com/capital-campaign-gift-range-chart/. Accessed 22 July 2021.

Kilbourne, Chris. Fire Drills: Why, When, and How - EHS Daily Advisor. EHS Daily Advisor, 21 Sept. 2010, ehsdailyadvisor.blr.com/2010/09/fire-drills-why-when-and-how/. Accessed 29 July 2021.

King, Stephen. Why Financial Management of a Nonprofit Is Harder than a For-Profit. Www.growthforce.com, www.growthforce.com/blog/why-financial-management-of-a-nonprofit-is-harder-than-running-a-for-profit. Accessed 13 July 2021.

Kurose, Stephanie. Requirements to Maintain 501(C)(3) Status. Info.legalzoom.com, info.legalzoom.com/article/requirements-maintain-501c3-status. Accessed 13 July 2021.

Lake, Laura. Marketing Strategies to Help Grow Your Nonprofit Organization. The Balance Small Business, 18 Sept. 2019, www.thebalancesmb.com/eight-easy-steps-to-marketing-your-nonprofit-organization-2294906. Accessed 28 July 2021.

Layne, Olivia. A Nonprofit's Guide to Risk Management - Nonprofit Hub. Nonprofit Hub, 17 July 2019, nonprofithub.org/resources/a-nonprofits-guide-to-risk-management/. Accessed 13 July 2021.

Lockwood Herman, Melanie. How to Hire the Staff Your Mission Deserves. Nonprofit Risk Management Center, nonprofitrisk.org/resources/articles/how-to-hire-the-staff-your-mission-deserves/. Accessed 19 July 2021.

Love, Jay. The Ultimate Guide to Nonprofit Strategic Planning. Bloomerang, 27 Mar. 2018, bloomerang.co/blog/the-ultimate-guide-to-nonprofit-strategic-planning/#:~:text=Nonprofit%20strategic%20planning%20is%20the. Accessed 28 July 2021.

Ludwig, Sean. 7 Things to Consider When Starting a Nonprofit. Https://Www.uschamber.com/Co, 2 Dec. 2020, www.uschamber.com/co/start/startup/starting-a-nonprofit-guide. Accessed 13 July 2021.

Mancuso, Anthony. How to Form a Nonprofit Corporation. Amazon, NOLO, 3 May 2019, www.amazon.com/Nonprofit-Corporation-National-Step-Step-ebook/dp/B07RF4S5XF/. Accessed 13 July 2021.

McNamara, Carter. All about Financial Management in Nonprofits. Managementhelp.org, 2019, managementhelp.org/nonprofitfinances/index.htm. Accessed 13 July 2021.

---. Basic Guide to Nonprofit Program Design and Marketing. Managementhelp.org, managementhelp.org/programmanagement/nonprofit-programs.htm. Accessed 13 July 2021.

---. Guidelines and Framework for Developing a Basic Logic Model. Managementhelp.org, 2019, managementhelp.org/freenonprofittraining/diagramming-your-nonprofit.htm. Accessed 28 July 2021.

---. Overview of Non-Profit Program Planning. Kent.edu, 2021,

literacy.kent.edu/Oasis/grants/overviewprogplan.html.
Accessed 13 July 2021.

McRay, Greg. Misappropriating Nonprofit Funds.
Foundation Group®, 23 Mar. 2017,
www.501c3.org/misappropriating-nonprofit-funds/.
Accessed 26 July 2021.

Miller, Judith. How to Manage Your Small Charity's
Finances - Top Tips. The Guardian, 7 May 2014,
www.theguardian.com/voluntary-sector-
network/2014/may/07/manage-small-charity-finances.
Accessed 13 July 2021.

Monson-Rosen, Madeleine. Understanding 5 Key Nonprofit
Financial Documents. MissionBox, 7 Mar. 2021,
www.missionbox.com/article/95/understanding-5-key-
nonprofit-financial-documents. Accessed 13 July 2021.

Moore, Sara. 5 Ways to Ensure Your Nonprofit's New
Name Hits the Mark. Mission Minded, 12 Dec. 2018,
mission-minded.com/5-ways-to-ensure-your-nonprofits-
new-name-hits-the-mark/. Accessed 30 July 2021.

Morand, Tatiana. How to Make Your Nonprofit Facebook
Page Great in under Five Hours. Wild Apricot Blog, 10 Jan.
2020, www.wildapricot.com/blog/facebook-for-nonprofits#1-
set-up-your-nonprofit-s-facebook-page. Accessed 21 July
2021.

---. How to Make Your Nonprofit Facebook Page Great in
under Five Hours. Wild Apricot Blog, 10 Jan. 2020,
www.wildapricot.com/blog/facebook-for-nonprofits#1-set-
up-your-nonprofit-s-facebook-page. Accessed 21 July
2021.

---. Twitter for Nonprofits: Does Your Organization Really
Need to Tweet? Wild Apricot Blog, 15 Jan. 2020,

www.wildapricot.com/blog/twitter-for-nonprofits. Accessed 22 July 2021.

Mostert, Cari. Your Nonprofit's Reputation and How to Protect It – Fundraising Ideas, Resources, and Letters. Fundraisingip.com, www.fundraisingip.com/fundraising/nonprofit-reputation-and-how-to-protect-it/. Accessed 13 July 2021.

National Council of Nonprofits. Nonprofit Audit Guide. National Council of Nonprofits, 14 Sept. 2018, www.councilofnonprofits.org/nonprofit-audit-guide. Accessed 13 July 2021.

Nonprofit Fundraising: A Complete Overview (20+ Methods!). Double the Donation, 2019, doublethedonation.com/tips/nonprofit-fundraising/. Accessed 13 July 2021.

Nonprofit Impact in Communities. National Council of Nonprofits, 22 Sept. 2014, www.councilofnonprofits.org/nonprofit-impact-communities#:~:text=They%20foster%20civic%20engagement%20and. Accessed 27 July 2021.

Nonprofit Risk Management Center. What Basic Insurance Coverage Should a Nonprofit Consider? Nonprofit Risk Management Center, nonprofitrisk.org/resources/e-news/what-basic-insurance-coverage-should-a-nonprofit-consider/. Accessed 29 July 2021.

Nonprofit Risk Management Santa Barbara - Nonprofit Kinect Consultants - Cynder Sinclair. Www.nonprofitkinect.org, www.nonprofitkinect.org/nonprofit-risk-management-santa-barbara. Accessed 29 July 2021.

Norris, Sean. 5 Small Tips for Big Nonprofit Growth. NonProfit PRO, 22 Nov. 2016, www.nonprofitpro.com/article/5-small-tips-big-nonprofit-growth/. Accessed 13 July 2021.

Not-For-Profits. Www.accountingfoundation.org, www.accountingfoundation.org/jsp/Foundation/Page/FAFBridgePage&cid=1176164540119. Accessed 26 July 2021.

Peri, Pakroo. Starting & Building a Nonprofit: A Practical Guide. Amazon, NOLO, 8 Feb. 2021, www.amazon.com/Starting-Building-Nonprofit-Practical-Guide-ebook/dp/B08PDR417B/. Accessed 13 July 2021.

Petermann, Christopher, et al. Using Financial Statements Together with IRS Form 990 to Understand Your Potential Grantees. Council of New Jersey Grantmakers, 20 June 2019, www.cnjg.org/sites/default/files/files/events/Presentation%20-%20Using%20Financial%20Statements%20Together%20with%20IRS%20Form%20990%20to%20Understand%20Your%20Potential%20Grantees.pdf. Accessed 23 July 2021.

Porteous, Chris. Should Your Business Be a for Profit or Nonprofit? Business.com, 10 Sept. 2020, www.business.com/articles/what-you-should-know-about-nonprofits/. Accessed 13 July 2021.

Price, Nick. Conflict of Interest Policy for Nonprofit Boards. BoardEffect, 18 Apr. 2018, www.boardeffect.com/blog/conflict-of-interest-policy-for-nonprofit-boards/. Accessed 13 July 2021.

Propel Nonprofits. 12 Golden Rules of Nonprofit Finance. Propel Nonprofits, 2017, www.propelnonprofits.org/resources/12-golden-rules-nonprofit-finance/. Accessed 13 July 2021.

Public Disclosure and Availability of Exempt Organizations Returns and Applications: Documents Subject to Public

Disclosure | Internal Revenue Service. Www.irs.gov, www.irs.gov/charities-non-profits/public-disclosure-and-availability-of-exempt-organizations-returns-and-applications-documents-subject-to-public-disclosure. Accessed 13 July 2021.

Public Disclosure Requirements for Nonprofits. National Council of Nonprofits, 12 Jan. 2015, www.councilofnonprofits.org/tools-resources/public-disclosure-requirements-nonprofits. Accessed 13 July 2021.

Rees, Sandy. The BEST Way to Find New Donors for Your Nonprofit. Get Fully Funded, 14 Jan. 2020, getfullyfunded.com/best-way-find-new-donors-nonprofit/. Accessed 13 July 2021.

Sanders, Aaron. How to Start, Run & Grow a Successful Nonprofit Organization: DIY Startup Guide to 501 C(3) Nonprofit Charitable Organization for All 50 States & DC. Amazon, Lost River Publishing House, 19 June 2018, www.amazon.com/Start-Grow-Successful-Nonprofit-Organization-ebook/dp/B07DW6GJZJ/. Accessed 13 July 2021.

Sandy Rees. 10 Growth Hacks for Small Nonprofits. Get Fully Funded, 6 Mar. 2018, getfullyfunded.com/10-growth-hacks-small-nonprofits/. Accessed 13 July 2021.

---. What You Need to Know Before You Start a Nonprofit. Get Fully Funded, 10 Sept. 2019, getfullyfunded.com/what-you-need-to-know-before-you-start-a-nonprofit/. Accessed 13 July 2021.

Sherman, Fraser. The Differences between a 501(C)(3) & Other Non-Profit Organizations. Small Business - Chron.com, 26 Aug. 2020, smallbusiness.chron.com/differences-between-501c3-

other-nonprofit-organizations-60190.html. Accessed 13 July 2021.

Small, Nick. Everything You Need to Know about Donor Relations. Nonprofit Hub, 8 June 2017, nonprofithub.org/donor-retention/donor-relations-everything-you-need/. Accessed 13 July 2021.

Staff Writer. Quiz: Should You Start a Nonprofit Business? Deluxe.com, Deluxe, 2021, www.deluxe.com/blog/should-you-start-nonprofit-quiz/. Accessed 13 July 2021.

Statement of Activities Definition. AccountingTools, 25 Feb. 2021, www.accountingtools.com/articles/2017/5/16/statement-of-activities. Accessed 26 July 2021.

The Difference between a Nonprofit Corporation and a 501(C)(3). Small Business - Chron.com, 25 Aug. 2020, smallbusiness.chron.com/difference-between-nonprofit-corporation-501c3-59719.html. Accessed 13 July 2021.

Thursday, et al. 9 Risk Management Strategies for Nonprofits. Jitasa Group, 12 Nov. 2020, www.jitasagroup.com/jitasa_nonprofit_blog/risk-management-for-nonprofits/. Accessed 13 July 2021.

---. Nonprofit Audits: A Complete Guide to Financial Auditing. Jitasa Group, 3 Dec. 2020, www.jitasagroup.com/jitasa_nonprofit_blog/nonprofit-audit/. Accessed 13 July 2021.

Trull, Hannah. 5 Motivational Quotes from Nonprofit Leaders (and How to Apply Them) - Nonprofit Hub. Nonprofit Hub, 24 May 2018, nonprofithub.org/nonprofit-marketing/motivational-quotes-from-nonprofit-leaders/. Accessed 27 Jan. 2020.

Tubbs, Freddie. How to Write a Compelling Fundraising
Letter. 18 Sept. 2018,
philanthropynewsdigest.org/columns/the-sustainable-
nonprofit/how-to-write-a-compelling-fundraising-letter.
Accessed 27 July 2021.

USPS.com FAQs. Usps.com, 2021,
faq.usps.com/s/article/What-is-Nonprofit-Mail. Accessed 15
July 2021.

What Are the Advantages/Disadvantages of Becoming a
Nonprofit Organization? Candid Learning,
learning.candid.org/resources/knowledge-base/pros-and-
cons/. Accessed 13 July 2021.

What Is a Standard Operating Procedure (SOP) [Includes
Template]. MaintainX, 9 Aug. 2019,
www.getmaintainx.com/what-is-a-standard-operating-
procedure-sop-includes-template/. Accessed 23 July 2021.

What Is Nonprofit Program Evaluation? Maryland
Nonprofits, 3 Apr. 2018, www.marylandnonprofits.org/what-
is-nonprofit-program-evaluation/. Accessed 13 July 2021.

Why Evaluation Is Important for Your Nonprofit. TSNE
MissionWorks, 1 Jan. 2019, www.tsne.org/blog/why-
evaluation-important-your-nonprofit. Accessed 13 July
2021.

Wilde, Heather. Council Post: Is a Nonprofit Right for Your
Business? Forbes, 17 Dec. 2019,
www.forbes.com/sites/forbestechcouncil/2019/12/17/is-a-
nonprofit-right-for-your-business/?sh=7b9a88da4bf4.
Accessed 13 July 2021.

Your 990 Made Simple: 5 Tips for Nonprofit Tax Filing -
Donorbox. Nonprofit Blog, 24 Apr. 2019,
donorbox.org/nonprofit-blog/your-990-made-simple/.
Accessed 13 July 2021.

www.ingramcontent.com/pod-product-compliance
Lightning Source LLC
Chambersburg PA
CBHW071554200326
41519CB00021BB/6745